VENDING MACHINE MASTERY

Your Guide to Success in a Thriving Industry

Traci Fischer

CONTENTS

Chapter 1: Introduction

In a world where time is a valuable commodity, convenience reigns supreme. We live in an age where the pace of life seems to accelerate daily, leaving little room for the leisurely activities of yesteryears. The need for instant gratification, coupled with busy schedules, has given rise to a burgeoning industry that caters to these demands, one quarter at a time – the vending machine business.

Picture this: you're rushing to catch a flight at the airport, and your stomach grumbles with hunger. There's no time to sit down at a restaurant, nor do you want to spend a fortune at the terminal's café. But, there, like an oasis in the desert, stands a vending machine, stocked with an array of snacks and beverages. You insert your coins, press a button, and voilà – a quick, satisfying solution to your hunger pangs.

The vending machine industry, though seemingly humble, has become an integral part of our daily lives. It provides not only sustenance on the go but also a means for entrepreneurs to tap into a reliable stream of income. With countless machines dispensing snacks, drinks, and other everyday essentials, this industry is ripe with opportunities for those who are willing to embark on a journey of entrepreneurship.

This book is your gateway into the exciting and profitable world of the vending machine business. Whether you're an aspiring entrepreneur looking for a low-cost, high-impact venture, or a seasoned businessperson seeking to diversify your investments, you'll find invaluable insights, guidance, and practical advice within these pages.

The vending machine business is more than just placing boxes of snacks in office break rooms or soda machines in school corridors. It's about understanding your market, selecting the right machines, navigating legal requirements, sourcing products, and managing operations efficiently. It's about devising clever pricing strategies, offering excellent customer service, and adapting to changing trends in consumer preferences. And it's about making a profit while doing so.

Throughout this book, you will taken on a comprehensive journey, starting with the basics and progressing to the advanced strategies that will set your vending business on a path to success. You'll learn how to research your market, choose the perfect vending machines, source products, maintain and repair your equipment, and keep your customers satisfied. We'll delve into the legal and regulatory aspects, as well as the financial and operational considerations that are vital for long-term sustainability.

The vending machine business is a dynamic field that continually evolves. As technology advances, so do opportunities for vending entrepreneurs. The latest trends such as cashless payment systems, environmentally friendly vending options will be explored, and even the potential for expanding your vending empire through franchising.

In the pages that follow, stories of successful vending machine business owners who have overcome challenges, realized their dreams, and turned vending machines into profitable enterprises will be shared. Their experiences and insights will inspire you and provide practical knowledge that can shape your own journey.

So, whether you're just beginning to explore the possibilities or already have machines in place, this book will be your trusted companion, guiding you through the intricacies of the vending machine business. The vending revolution is here, and you can be part of it. Let's embark on this journey together, unlocking the potential of this remarkable industry and turning your vending dreams into reality.

Chapter 2: Market Research – Paving the Path to Vending Success

Imagine setting up a vending machine that dispenses health-conscious snacks in a bustling shopping mall, only to realize that your target customers are more inclined towards sugary indulgences. Or, picture investing in a row of vending machines in a quiet neighbourhood, not knowing that a school nearby is your potential goldmine. Such scenarios can spell the difference between vending triumph and disaster. In the vending machine business, knowledge is power, and your roadmap to success begins with thorough market research.

Market research is not just a preliminary step; it's an ongoing practice that can make or break your venture. By the end of this chapter, you'll be equipped with the skills and knowledge to make informed decisions that will lay a solid foundation for your vending business.

❖ Understanding the Vending Machine Market

Before you embark on your vending journey, it's essential to have a comprehensive understanding of the vending machine market. The vending industry is not one-size-fits-all; it spans various niches, each with its own set of opportunities and challenges.

Types of Vending Machines

Vending machines come in different forms, catering to a variety of products. Here are some common types:

1. **Snack Vending Machines**: These machines dispense a range of snacks, from chips and candies to healthier options like granola bars and dried fruits.

2. **Beverage Vending Machines**: These machines provide an assortment of drinks, including sodas, bottled water, energy drinks, and coffee.

3. **Combo Vending Machines**: These versatile machines offer both snacks and beverages in one unit, making them suitable for locations with limited space.

4. **Healthy Vending Machines**: Focused on providing nutritious choices, these machines

5. offer items like fresh fruit, yogurt, and organic snacks.

6. **Specialty Vending Machines**: These cater to niche markets, such as vending art supplies in an art school or electronic gadgets in an airport.

7. **Hot Food Vending Machines**: Some machines are designed to heat and serve hot meals like pizza slices, sandwiches, or even gourmet items.

8. **Ice Cream Vending Machines**: Ideal for parks, beaches, and other outdoor locations, these machines dispense frozen treats.

9. **Laundry Detergent Vending Machines**: Found in laundromats, they provide laundry essentials.

10. **Medicine Vending Machines**: Often seen in hospitals or clinics, these machines offer over-the-counter medications.

Understanding the types of vending machines available allows you to make an informed choice regarding the niche that best suits your business goals and the needs of your target market.

❖ Vending Machine Locations

The success of your vending business is closely tied to the locations of your machines. Vending machines can be strategically placed in a wide array of settings. Here are some common locations:

1. **Schools and Universities**: From elementary schools to college campuses, educational institutions are prime locations for snack and beverage vending machines.

2. **Office Buildings**: Employees often appreciate the convenience of vending machines for a quick snack or drink during their workday.

3. **Hospitals and Healthcare Facilities**: Waiting rooms and cafeterias in medical facilities can benefit from vending machines.

4. **Airports and Transportation Hubs**: High foot traffic areas like airports, bus stations, and train stations are excellent locations for vending machines.

5. **Malls and Shopping Centres**: Retail spaces attract a diverse crowd, making them ideal for various types of vending machines.

6. **Gyms and Fitness Centres**: Health-conscious customers at fitness centers may appreciate healthy vending options.

7. **Manufacturing Plants**: Factories and manufacturing facilities often have on-site vending machines for employees.

8. **Hotels**: Hotels may have vending machines on different floors or in common areas for guests' convenience.

9. **Laundromats**: Vending machines selling snacks and laundry supplies can be profitable in laundromats.

10. **Apartment Complexes:** Common areas in residential buildings can be excellent locations for vending machines.

11. **Entertainment Venues:** Consider placing machines in cinemas, theatres, amusement parks, and concert halls.

12. **Public Buildings:** Government buildings, libraries, and municipal offices can house vending machines for visitors.

Each location has its unique characteristics, and your choice should align with your target market.
For example, if you're targeting health-conscious individuals, gyms and fitness centres might be a prime location. On the other hand, if you aim to serve a diverse audience, shopping malls and

airports could be more suitable.

❖ Identifying Your Target Market

Now that you have a grasp of the vending landscape, it's time to pinpoint your target market. Your target market is the group of people most likely to use your vending machines. Understanding their needs, preferences, and behaviours is the key to tailoring your offerings effectively.

⬜ Demographics

Demographics are an essential starting point for defining your target market. Consider factors such as age, gender, income level, and education. Are you catering to students, working professionals, families, or seniors? For instance, if you plan to place vending machines in a university, your target demographic might be students between the ages of 18 and 24.

☐ Psychographics

Psychographics delve deeper into your target market's psychology. What are their values, lifestyles, and interests? Do they prioritize convenience, health, or indulgence? For example, if you're aiming to serve health-conscious individuals, you'll need to offer nutritious snacks and beverages that align with their values.

☐ Location-Based Factors

The location of your vending machines can also influence your target market. A machine in a busy airport will attract a different audience compared to one in a small suburban office building. Consider the local population, their preferences, and purchasing power.

□ Behavioural Insights

Analysing consumer behaviour is vital. What are the buying habits of your target market? Do they make impulse purchases, or are they more price-sensitive? Do they prefer cash transactions, or are they inclined towards digital payments? Gaining insights into these behaviours will help you stock your machines appropriately and set competitive prices.

□ Competitor Analysis

In addition to studying your potential customers, it's crucial to analyze your competitors. Identify other vending businesses operating in your chosen niche and location. What products are they offering? What is their pricing strategy? Are they meeting the needs of the target market effectively, or are there gaps you can exploit?

☐ Survey and Feedback

One of the most effective ways to gain insights into your target market is through surveys and feedback. Engage with potential customers in your chosen locations and ask for their input. You can also launch online surveys or collect feedback through your vending machines. Listen to what people have to say, and use their input to refine your offerings.

Market research is not a one-time effort. It's an ongoing process that should adapt as your business evolves and customer preferences change. By understanding your target market inside and out, you'll be better equipped to make informed decisions about product selection, pricing, and

location placement.

❖ **Analysing the Competition**

Competitor analysis is a critical component of your market research. It provides you with a clear picture of your business landscape, allowing you to identify opportunities, anticipate challenges, and develop strategies to stand out. Here's how to effectively analyze the competition in the vending machine industry:

☐ Identify Your Competitors

Start by identifying who your direct and indirect competitors are. Direct competitors are those vending machine businesses that offer similar products or services in the same locations or locations similar to your target market. Indirect competitors might not offer the exact same products but cater to a similar audience or locations.

☐ Product and Service Offerings

Analyse what products and services your competitors offer. Are they focusing on snacks, beverages, or a combination of both? Are there any unique items or niche products in their vending machines? Understanding their offerings will help you differentiate your business.

☐ Pricing Strategies

Examine the pricing strategies employed by your competitors. Are they priced competitively, or do they cater to premium markets with higher prices? It's important to strike a balance between offering value to your customers while maintaining profitability.

 Machine Quality and Technology

Assess the quality and technology of your competitors' vending machines. Are they using modern, reliable machines with advanced features like cashless payment options and real-time inventory tracking? Upgrading your machines or adopting new technology can give you a competitive edge.

 Location Placement

Study the locations where your competitors have placed their vending machines. Are they concentrated in specific areas, or have they covered a broad range of locations? Identifying locations with high foot traffic that your competitors have missed can be a strategic move.

☐ Customer Reviews and Feedback

Check customer reviews and feedback about your competitors. What are customers saying about the quality of products, machine reliability, and customer service? Use this information to identify areas where you can outperform your competition.

☐ Market Trends and Innovations

Stay up-to-date with market trends and innovations in the vending machine industry. Are there emerging products or technologies that your competitors haven't adopted yet? Being an early adopter can set you apart from the competition.

☐ SWOT Analysis

Perform a SWOT (Strengths, Weaknesses, Opportunities, Threats) analysis for each of your competitors. Identify their strengths that you can learn from, their weaknesses that you can capitalize on, the opportunities they might have missed, and the potential threats to their business.

  ☐ Unique Selling Proposition (USP)

Now that you have a good understanding of your competitors, it's time to define your Unique Selling Proposition (USP). What makes your vending machine business stand out from the rest? It could be a unique product offering, exceptional customer service, or innovative technology. Your USP is what will attract customers and keep them coming back.

❖ Scouting for Ideal Locations

Once you've gained insights into your target market and competitors, the next step is scouting for the best locations to place your vending machines. Location is one of the most critical factors in the success of your vending business. Here's how to find and secure prime locations:

- Foot Traffic and Demographics

Look for locations with high foot traffic that match your target market's demographics. Places like schools, offices, transportation hubs, and shopping centres can offer substantial customer traffic. Analyse the age groups, income levels, and preferences of people frequenting these locations.

- Local Regulations and Permits

Check local regulations and permit requirements for vending machines. Some locations may have restrictions or licensing requirements. Ensure that you comply with all legal and regulatory obligations before placing your machines.

- Site Agreements

To secure a location for your vending machine, you'll often need to negotiate site agreements with property owners or managers. These agreements can vary widely, so be prepared to negotiate terms, such as rental fees, profit-sharing arrangements, and the duration of the placement.

- Competitive Analysis in Locations

Consider the competition in potential locations. If a particular site already has several vending machines offering similar products, you might face fierce competition. However, if you can offer unique products or better terms to the location owner, you might still find success.

Visibility and Accessibility

Ensure that your vending machines are highly visible and easily accessible to your target customers. A machine tucked away in a corner may not attract as much attention as one placed in a prominent, well-lit spot.

 Security and Safety

Evaluate the security and safety of potential locations. You want to ensure the safety of your machines, as well as the safety of customers who use them. High-crime areas may require additional security measures.

 Trial Periods

In some cases, it's a good idea to negotiate trial periods with location owners. This allows you to test the performance of your vending machines in a particular location before committing to a long-term agreement.

☐ Expansion Plans

Consider the scalability of your vending business. Are there opportunities for expanding within the same location, or are there nearby locations where you can place additional machines? Having a clear expansion strategy is crucial for long-term growth.

☐ Local Events and Seasons

Take into account local events and seasons that may impact customer traffic. For example, if you're placing machines near a convention centre, events can significantly boost sales during conferences and exhibitions.

☐ Customer Feedback

Engage with customers in potential locations to gather feedback on what they'd like to see in vending machines. This can help you tailor your offerings to local preferences.

❖ The Power of Data and Analytics

In today's digital age, data and analytics play a pivotal role in market research and location scouting. You can leverage technology to collect valuable data that can inform your decisions. Consider the following:

☐ Machine Telemetry

Many modern vending machines come equipped with telemetry systems that provide real-time data on sales, inventory levels, and machine performance.

This data can help you make informed restocking decisions and track the popularity of specific products.

☐ Cashless Payment Data

If you accept cashless payments, you can analyse transaction data to gain insights into customer behaviour. It allows you to understand purchasing patterns, peak sales times, and preferred payment methods.

☐ Customer Surveys

Collect feedback from customers through surveys and interactive screens on your vending machines. Ask them about product preferences, pricing, and the overall vending experience. This data can guide product selection and pricing strategies.

☐ Website and Social Media Analytics

If you have a website or social media presence for your vending business, analyse web traffic and social media engagement. This can provide additional insights into customer interests and preferences.

Remember that market research and location scouting are ongoing processes. Even after you've placed your vending machines, continue to collect and analyse data to adapt to changing market conditions and customer needs. Your ability to make data-driven decisions will be a key factor in your vending business's success.

❖ Case Study: Maximizing Location Potential

To illustrate the significance of careful location selection, let's delve into a case study of a vending machine business owner who harnessed the power of market research and strategic location placement.

Case Study: Smart Snacks Vending

Meet Jane, a savvy entrepreneur who launched "Smart Snacks Vending," a vending machine business specializing in healthier snack options. Jane recognized the growing trend of health-conscious consumers and saw an opportunity to provide nutritious alternatives in the vending market.

Market Research and Target Market: Jane conducted extensive market research and identified her target market as health-conscious individuals, including gym-goers, office workers looking for healthier options, and students at local universities.

Competitor Analysis: Jane studied her competition and observed that most vending machines in her area primarily offered traditional snacks with few healthy choices.

Strategic Location Selection: Jane decided to strategically place her vending machines in locations that aligned with her target market. She secured agreements with two local gyms, an office building, and a university campus.

Site Agreements: Jane negotiated rental agreements with the gym owners, the office building management, and the university campus authorities. Her agreements included a profit-sharing arrangement where she shared a percentage of her vending machine earnings with the location owners.

Data and Analytics: Jane invested in vending machines equipped with telemetry systems, allowing her to monitor sales and inventory levels in real-time. She also encouraged customers to provide feedback through digital surveys on the vending machine screens.

Success and Expansion: Jane's vending machines quickly gained popularity in their locations. Customers appreciated the convenient access to healthy snacks, and the data collected from telemetry and customer feedback guided her product selection. Jane eventually expanded her business to additional gyms, yoga studios, and even local health clinics.

Lesson Learned: By conducting thorough market research, identifying her target market, analysing competitors, and strategically placing her vending machines, Jane maximized the potential of her locations. Her data-driven approach ensured that she continued to meet her customers' needs and expand her business successfully.

◆ Key Takeaways

In this chapter, you've learned the importance of market research in starting and growing your vending machine business. Here are the key takeaways:

1. Understand the vending machine market, including the various types of machines and their applications.

2. Identify your target market by analysing demographics, psychographics, location-based factors, and customer behaviour.

3. Conduct a thorough competitor analysis to understand your competition's strengths, weaknesses, and strategies.

4. Scout for ideal locations by considering foot traffic, local regulations, site agreements, and competitive analysis.

5. Leverage data and analytics to make informed decisions and adapt to changing market conditions.

6. Your ability to select the right locations for your vending machines can significantly impact your business's success.

Market research is an ongoing process, and it's essential to stay attuned to your customers' preferences and evolving market trends.

Chapter 3: Choosing the Right Vending Machines – Your Gateway to Success

As you embark on your journey into the vending machine business, one of the most pivotal decisions you'll make is selecting the right vending machines for your venture. The types of machines you choose, whether for snacks, beverages, healthy options, or a combination of these, can significantly influence your profitability, customer satisfaction, and overall success.

❖ Types of Vending Machines

Vending machines come in a variety of types, each designed to cater to different consumer needs and preferences. Understanding the options available is essential to make an informed decision that aligns with your business goals. Let's explore some of the most common types of vending machines:

1. Snack Vending Machines

Snack vending machines are ubiquitous, offering a wide range of snacks to satisfy people's cravings. They can dispense items like chips, candies, chocolates, nuts, and pastries. These machines are popular in schools, offices, and locations where people seek quick, convenient snacks.

2. Beverage Vending Machines

Beverage vending machines are designed to provide a variety of drinks, including soda, bottled water, energy drinks, and even hot beverages like coffee or tea. They're commonly found in schools, office buildings, hospitals, and public areas with high foot traffic.

3. Combo Vending Machines

Combo vending machines are versatile units that offer both snacks and beverages in a single machine. These machines are ideal for locations with limited space, as they allow customers to choose from a wider selection of products in one place.

4. Healthy Vending Machines

As the demand for healthier snack options grows, healthy vending machines have become increasingly popular. These machines dispense items such as fresh fruit, yogurt, protein bars, and organic snacks. They are often found in fitness centres, schools, and health-conscious workplaces.

5. Specialty Vending Machines

Specialty vending machines cater to niche markets and specific product categories. They can include machines that dispense art supplies in art schools, electronic gadgets in airports, or even live bait in fishing locations. These machines require careful consideration of the unique needs of their target audience.

6. Hot Food Vending Machines

Hot food vending machines are designed to heat and serve a variety of hot meals, from pizza slices and sandwiches to more gourmet options. They're often placed in locations like convenience stores, offices, and outdoor events.

7. Ice Cream Vending Machines

Ice cream vending machines are perfect for warm-weather locations, such as parks, beaches, and outdoor events. They dispense frozen treats in a range of flavours.

8. Laundry Detergent Vending Machines

These machines are typically found in laundromats and provide customers with essential laundry supplies, such as detergent and fabric softener.

9. Medicine Vending Machines

Commonly placed in healthcare facilities, these machines offer over-the-counter medications and health products. They provide convenience for patients and visitors.

Selecting the right type of vending machine is a crucial initial step. It will depend on your target market, the products you plan to offer, and the locations where you intend to place them. Your choice of vending machine type should align with the needs and preferences of your customers.

❖ New vs. Used Vending Machines

Once you've decided on the type of vending machine that suits your business model, the next choice you'll face is whether to purchase new or used machines. Both options have their advantages and drawbacks, and your decision will depend on various factors, including your budget, business goals, and risk tolerance.

❖ New Vending Machines

Advantages:

Reliability: New machines typically come with warranties, providing peace of mind regarding their performance and durability.

Up-to-Date Features: New machines often incorporate the latest technology, such as cashless payment systems and energy-efficient components.

Customization: You can choose the specific model and features that best suit your business needs.

Fresh Appearance: New machines have a polished and modern appearance that can attract customers.

Drawbacks:

Higher Cost: New vending machines are more expensive than used ones, which can significantly impact your initial investment.

Depreciation: The value of a new machine depreciates rapidly, potentially affecting your resale value if you decide to upgrade or sell the machines.

Limited History: Since they are new, you won't have historical data on their performance in specific locations.

❖ **Used Vending Machines**

Advantages:

Lower Cost: Used machines are more budget-friendly, reducing your initial investment.

Proven Track Record: You can assess the historical performance of used machines in their previous locations, helping you make informed decisions.

Quick Deployment: You can start your vending business more swiftly by purchasing and deploying used machines.

Drawbacks:

Potential Maintenance Issues: Used machines may require more frequent maintenance or repairs, which can increase operational costs.

Limited Warranty: Used machines may not come with warranties, so you bear the responsibility for any repairs.

Obsolete Technology: Older machines may lack the latest features and payment options, potentially affecting customer satisfaction.

The choice between new and used vending machines depends on your available budget, risk tolerance, and how quickly you want to start your business. If you opt for used machines, thorough inspections and maintenance before deployment are crucial to

ensure their reliability and functionality.

❖ Machine Specifications and Features

When selecting vending machines, you'll need to consider their specifications and features to meet your business needs. Here are some key factors to evaluate:

☐ Capacity

Determine the machine's capacity, which includes the number of product slots and the quantity of items each slot can hold. For example, a snack vending machine may have several rows of shelves, with each shelf accommodating different snacks. Be sure to choose machines with sufficient capacity to meet customer demand while minimizing restocking frequency.

◻ Product Compatibility

Ensure that the machine you select can accommodate the specific products you intend to sell. Different vending machines are designed for various product sizes and shapes, so check that your products fit comfortably in the available slots.

◻ Temperature Control

If you plan to offer perishable items or beverages, it's essential to select vending machines with adequate temperature control. Some machines have built-in refrigeration or heating systems to keep products at the desired temperature, ensuring their freshness and quality.

☐ Payment Options

Consider the payment options available with your vending machines. Modern machines often accept a range of payment methods, including cash, coins, credit and debit cards, mobile payments, and even cryptocurrency. Providing multiple payment options can attract a more diverse customer base.

☐ Digital Screens and Displays

Vending machines with digital screens and displays offer opportunities for interactive engagement with customers. These screens can be used to display product information, advertisements, promotions, and even customer feedback surveys.

Telemetry and Remote Monitoring

Telemetry systems allow you to monitor your vending machines remotely. You can track sales, inventory levels, and machine status in real-time. This data-driven approach can help you make informed restocking decisions and assess machine performance.

  Energy Efficiency

Consider the energy efficiency of your vending machines. Energy-efficient machines not only help reduce operational costs but also align with sustainability goals. Look for machines with Energy Star certification or similar energy-efficient features.

☐ Security Features

Vending machines often house valuable products and cash, making security a top concern. Look for features such as sturdy locks, tamper-resistant designs, and security cameras to protect your machines from theft and vandalism.

☐ Serviceability

Ease of maintenance is a critical consideration. Machines that are designed for easy access to internal components and have user-friendly interfaces can reduce downtime and maintenance costs.

☐ Warranty and Support

If you opt for new machines, check the warranty and support options provided by the manufacturer.

A robust warranty and access to customer support can provide peace of mind and timely assistance if issues

arise.

 ⬜ Aesthetics and Customization

The appearance of your vending machines can influence customer perception. Some machines offer customizable exteriors, allowing you to brand them with your logo and colors. A well-designed machine can attract more customers and enhance your brand image.

 ⬜ Location Placement Considerations

When selecting vending machines, keep in mind the specific requirements of the locations where you plan to place them. For example, if you intend to place machines in a gym, you'll want machines that offer healthy snacks and beverages. Understanding the preferences and needs of each location's clientele is essential for your machine's success.

❖ **Key Factors to Consider When Choosing Vending Machines**

To ensure that you make the best choice when selecting vending machines for your business, consider the following key factors:

1. Target Market Compatibility

Your choice of vending machines should align with the preferences and needs of your target market. If you're targeting health-conscious individuals, opt for machines that offer nutritious snacks and beverages. Understanding your customers' preferences is crucial.

2. Location Requirements

Different locations have varying needs and space constraints. Ensure that your vending machines fit the available space and offer the right product mix. For example, an office building might benefit from combo machines, while a school may require snack and beverage machines.

3. Budget Constraints

Your budget will play a significant role in your decision-making process. Consider the cost of the vending machines, whether you're purchasing new or used units, and the available funds for initial investment.

4. Long-Term Maintenance and Support

Evaluate the long-term maintenance requirements

and availability of support for your chosen vending machines. Machines with good warranty coverage and reliable customer support can save you time and money in the long run.

5. Payment Options

Consider the payment methods that your machines will accept. Modern machines offer a variety of payment options, from cash and coins to credit cards and mobile payments. Providing multiple options can attract a broader customer base.

6. Energy Efficiency

Opt for energy-efficient machines to reduce operational costs and minimize your environmental footprint. Energy-efficient vending machines are not only cost-effective but also contribute to sustainability efforts.

Telemetry and Data Tracking

If you plan to scale your vending business and want to monitor machine performance remotely, consider machines equipped with telemetry systems. Real-time data tracking can help you make informed decisions and optimize your operations.

Security Measures

Vending machines can be vulnerable to theft and vandalism. Choose machines with robust security features, such as durable locks and tamper-resistant designs, to protect your investments.

Customization and Branding

If branding and aesthetics are important to your business, look for machines that offer customization options. This allows you to brand your machines with your logo and colors, enhancing your brand image.

❖ Case Study: Smart Choices Vending's Machine Selection Strategy

To illustrate the importance of choosing the right vending machines, let's explore a case study of "Smart Choices Vending," a successful vending business that carefully considered its machine selection strategy.

Case Study: Smart Choices Vending

Smart Choices Vending, owned by Mark, is a vending machine business that focuses on offering healthy snack and beverage options. Mark recognized the growing demand for nutritious products and decided to target locations with health-conscious customers.

Machine Selection: Mark decided to invest in new, state-of-the-art vending machines with energy-efficient refrigeration units. These machines had multiple temperature zones to ensure the freshness of products. He also chose machines with digital screens for interactive engagement with customers and telemetry systems for real-time data tracking.

Product Compatibility: Mark selected vending machines specifically designed for the sizes and shapes of the healthy snacks and beverages he planned to offer. The machines had adjustable shelving to accommodate a variety of product types.

Location Requirements: Mark carefully assessed each location's space and product requirements. In fitness centres, he placed combo vending machines with a mix of healthy snacks and beverages. In office buildings, he deployed snack and beverage machines tailored to suit the tastes of working professionals.

Budget Constraints: Mark understood the importance of managing costs. While he invested in new machines with warranties, he also explored financing options to spread the initial investment over time.

Long-Term Maintenance and Support: Mark established relationships with vending machine manufacturers that offered reliable customer support. He also implemented a proactive maintenance schedule to ensure his machines operated smoothly.

Payment Options: Mark's vending machines accepted various payment methods, including cash, coins, credit and debit cards, and mobile payments. This flexibility catered to a broad range of customers.

Energy Efficiency: Mark's machines were chosen for their energy-efficient features, which not only reduced operational costs but also aligned with his business's sustainability goals.

Security Measures: Security was a top priority for Mark. He equipped his machines with durable locks and installed security cameras in certain locations to deter theft and vandalism.

Customization and Branding: Mark took advantage of the customization options offered by the vending machine manufacturer, allowing him to brand his machines with the Smart Choices Vending logo and colours.

Outcome: Smart Choices Vending became a recognized brand in the vending industry, known for its commitment to health-conscious offerings and customer satisfaction. Mark's strategic machine selection contributed significantly to the company's success.

❖ Key Takeaways

In this chapter, you've explored the critical process of choosing the right vending machines for your business. Here are the key takeaways:

1. Understand the different types of vending machines available and their applications, including snack, beverage, combo, healthy, specialty, hot food, and more.

2. Decide between new and used vending machines, considering factors like reliability, budget, and available support.

3. Evaluate machine specifications and features, including capacity, product compatibility, temperature control, payment options, digital screens, telemetry, and energy efficiency.

4. Choose vending machines that align with your target market's preferences and location requirements.

5. Budget constraints, long-term maintenance and support, payment options, energy efficiency, security measures, customization, and branding should all be considered when selecting vending machines.

Your choice of vending machines is a pivotal step that will impact your vending business's performance and profitability. By aligning your machine selection with the needs of your target market and locations, you're setting a solid foundation for success.

Chapter 4: Legal and Regulatory Considerations for Your Vending Machine Business

As you build your vending machine business, it's essential to navigate the complex landscape of legal and regulatory requirements. These rules and regulations are in place to protect consumers, maintain health and safety standards, and ensure fair competition. Understanding and complying with these laws is critical to the success of your venture.

❖ Licensing and Permits

Before you start your vending machine business, you'll need to secure the necessary licenses and permits. The specific requirements can vary based on your location, the types of products you sell, and the scale of your operation. Here are the key licenses and permits to consider:

☐ Business License

A general business license is typically required to operate any business, including a vending machine business. This license is issued by your local city or county government and ensures that your business complies with local regulations.

☐ Vending Machine Operator License

Some jurisdictions may require a vending machine operator license, which is specific to the vending industry. This license ensures that operators meet certain standards related to the operation, maintenance, and placement of vending machines.

☐ Health Department Permits

If you plan to sell food or beverages in your vending machines, you'll need health department permits. These permits ensure that you adhere to food safety and hygiene standards. The specific requirements and inspections can vary, so check with your local health department.

☐ Sales Tax Permit

In many regions, you're required to collect and remit sales tax on the products you sell through your vending machines. To do this, you'll need a sales tax permit, which allows you to legally collect and report sales tax to the appropriate government agency.

☐ Zoning Permits

Zoning regulations can affect where you're allowed to place your vending machines. Check with your local zoning department to ensure that your vending machine placement complies with zoning laws.

☐ State-Specific Requirements

Some states have specific vending machine regulations and requirements. For instance, in California, vending machines must meet certain nutritional guidelines if placed in public schools. Be sure to research any state-specific regulations that apply to your business.

☐ Federal Regulations

Federal regulations may also apply, especially if you plan to sell products across state lines or have a large-scale vending operation. The U.S. Food and Drug Administration (FDA) and the Federal Trade Commission (FTC) have regulations that can affect certain vending products.

It's crucial to research the specific licensing and permit requirements in your area and ensure that your vending machine business complies with all relevant regulations. Failure to obtain the necessary licenses and permits can result in fines and legal complications.

❖ Product Labelling and Nutrition Information

If your vending machines offer food or beverages, you'll need to comply with product labeling and nutrition information requirements. These regulations are primarily aimed at ensuring that consumers have access to accurate and transparent information about the products they purchase. Here are some key considerations:

☐ Nutrition Facts Labels

The FDA requires that most packaged food products have a Nutrition Facts label that provides detailed information about the product's nutritional content. This label includes information about calories, serving sizes, fat content, carbohydrates, and more.

☐ Allergen Information

If your vending machine products contain any of the major food allergens (such as peanuts, tree nuts, milk, eggs, soy, wheat, fish, or shellfish), you must clearly label these allergens on the product packaging.

- Ingredient List

An ingredient list should be included on the product packaging, listing all the ingredients in descending order of prominence. This helps consumers with food allergies or dietary restrictions.

- Country of Origin Labelling

Certain products, like fresh produce and meats, must include country of origin labeling. It informs consumers about the source of the product, which can be important for food safety and quality.

- Calorie Labelling on Menus and Vending Machines

The Affordable Care Act requires that vending machine operators with 20 or more machines that sell food and beverages offer calorie information for their products. This requirement helps consumers make informed choices about what they purchase.

It's crucial to work with suppliers who provide accurate and compliant labelling for the products you intend to sell in your vending machines. Additionally, ensure that your vending machines display the required calorie information as mandated by the law.

❖ **Product Safety and Quality Standards**

Vending machine operators must ensure that the products they offer meet safety and quality standards. These standards vary depending on the type of products you sell, but they generally cover the following areas:

☐ Food Safety

If you sell food products, you must adhere to food safety regulations. This includes proper storage, handling, and temperature control of perishable items. Regular cleaning and maintenance of your vending machines to prevent contamination are also essential.

☐ Beverage Safety

Beverage vending machines should maintain the integrity of the beverages they dispense. Ensuring that the products are not tampered with, and that the machines are sanitary, is essential.

☐ Product Quality

Products should meet established quality standards to ensure that consumers receive what they expect.

For instance, if you sell beverages, they should be properly mixed, and if you sell snacks, they should not be stale or expired.

Certifications

Some products may require specific certifications, such as organic or kosher certifications. Ensure that any required certifications are in place for the products you sell.

It's critical to establish processes and procedures for regularly inspecting, cleaning, and maintaining your vending machines. Additionally, work with suppliers and distributors that adhere to safety and quality standards to provide reliable products to your customers.

❖ Compliance with Accessibility Laws

Vending machine operators need to ensure that their machines are accessible to all customers, including those with disabilities. Accessibility laws, such as the Americans with Disabilities Act (ADA) in the United States, require that certain accommodations be made. Here are some key considerations:

☐ Accessible Route to Vending Machines

Ensure that there is an accessible route to your vending machines that accommodates customers with mobility impairments, such as those using wheelchairs.

Reach Range

Vending machines should have controls and features that are within reach of customers with disabilities. The height and positioning of buttons and coin slots should be accessible to all customers.

 Clear Floor Space

Provide a clear floor space in front of vending machines so that customers with mobility devices can easily approach and access the machines.

 Braille and Tactile Signs

Incorporate Braille and tactile signs on or near your vending machines to assist customers with visual impairments.

Audio Features

Consider offering audio features on your vending machines, such as auditory instructions and information about product selection. This can be valuable for customers with visual or cognitive impairments.

 Compliance Reporting

Some regulations may require operators to maintain records or reports demonstrating compliance with accessibility laws. Be prepared to document your efforts to ensure accessibility for all customers.

It's essential to conduct a comprehensive assessment of your vending machine locations to ensure compliance with accessibility laws. Consult with accessibility experts or authorities to make any necessary adjustments to your machines to accommodate all customers.

❖ Taxation and Reporting

Taxes and financial reporting are an integral part of operating any business, including a vending machine business. Properly managing your taxes and financial reporting is not only a legal requirement but also a crucial aspect of maintaining the financial health of your venture. Here are some important considerations:

☐ Sales Tax Collection and Reporting

As mentioned earlier, you may be required to collect and remit sales tax on the products you sell. Ensure that you are collecting the correct amount of sales tax and that you report and remit it to the appropriate tax authorities on time.

☐ Income Tax Reporting

Vending machine operators are subject to income tax on their business earnings. Accurate financial records and tax reporting are essential for compliance.

☐ Recordkeeping

Maintain detailed records of your income and expenses related to your vending machine business. Proper recordkeeping not only ensures compliance but also helps you manage your finances more effectively.

☐ Employment Taxation

If you have employees in your vending machine business, you'll need to comply with employment tax obligations, including withholding and remitting payroll taxes.

☐ Local Taxes

In addition to state and federal taxes, some local jurisdictions may impose additional taxes or fees on vending machine operators. Be aware of local tax requirements in your area.

☐ Consult with a Tax Professional

Tax laws and regulations can be complex and subject to change. It's highly advisable to consult with a tax professional or accountant who can help you navigate the tax implications of your vending machine business and ensure full compliance.

❖ **Consumer Protection and Advertising**

Your vending machine business should adhere to consumer protection laws, which are designed to safeguard consumers from deceptive practices. Here are some key considerations:

☐ Truth in Advertising

Ensure that any advertising or marketing materials associated with your vending machines are truthful and not misleading. Avoid false claims or exaggerations about the products you offer.

☐ Pricing Transparency

Clearly display prices for your products on or near the vending machines. Ensure that customers are aware of the cost before making a purchase.

☐ Product Recalls

Stay informed about product recalls, especially if you sell food or beverages. If a product in your vending machine is subject to a recall, take prompt action to remove it from circulation.

- Customer Complaints

Establish a process for handling customer complaints or concerns. Address any issues or disputes promptly and professionally.

- Compliance with Labelling Laws

Ensure that your products are labelled in compliance with all applicable laws and regulations, as discussed earlier.

❖ **Environmental Regulations**

Vending machine operators should also be aware of environmental regulations, particularly if their machines use refrigeration or other energy-intensive processes. Here are some considerations:

- Refrigerant Management

If your vending machines use refrigeration, be aware

of regulations related to refrigerant gases, as certain refrigerants can harm the environment if not managed properly.

□ Energy Efficiency

Consider investing in energy-efficient vending machines to reduce your environmental impact and operating costs.

□ Recycling and Waste Management

Establish procedures for recycling or proper disposal of materials used in your vending machine business, such as product packaging and machine components.

□ Compliance with Local Environmental Regulations

Local governments may have specific environmental regulations that affect vending machine operations. Ensure that your business complies with these regulations.

❖ Insurance

Insurance is an essential component of managing the risks associated with your vending machine business. While insurance requirements can vary, here are some types of insurance you should consider:

□ General Liability Insurance

This insurance provides coverage in case of accidents or injuries that occur on the premises where your vending machines are located. It can also protect you from claims of property damage or negligence.

□ Product Liability Insurance

If a product sold through your vending machines causes harm to a customer, product liability insurance can provide coverage for legal claims related to the product's safety or quality.

☐ Property Insurance

Property insurance protects your vending machines and inventory from damage due to events like fire, vandalism, or theft.

☐ Business Interruption Insurance

Business interruption insurance can provide financial protection if your vending machines are temporarily unable to operate due to unforeseen circumstances, such as a natural disaster.

☐ Workers' Compensation Insurance

If you have employees, workers' compensation insurance is typically required to provide coverage in case of employee injuries or illnesses on the job.

Auto Insurance

If you use vehicles for your vending machine operations, commercial auto insurance may be necessary to cover accidents or damage related to your vehicles.

Insurance requirements can vary depending on your location, the products you sell, and your business structure. Consult with an insurance agent to determine the most suitable coverage for your vending machine business.

❖ Contractual Agreements

In addition to regulatory and legal considerations, contractual agreements play a significant role in the operation of your vending machine business. These agreements establish the terms and conditions under which you operate with property owners and suppliers. Key contractual agreements include:

☐ Site Agreements

Site agreements are contracts between you and the owners or managers of the locations where your vending machines are placed. These agreements outline the terms of machine placement, rental fees, profit-sharing arrangements, and other conditions specific to each location.

☐ Supplier Contracts

Supplier contracts are crucial if you source your products from external vendors. These contracts establish the terms of product supply, including pricing, delivery schedules, and quality standards.

Service and Maintenance Agreements

If you work with service providers for machine maintenance and restocking, having service and maintenance agreements in place can clarify the terms of service, response times, and costs.

 Financial Agreements

If you secure financing or loans to support your vending machine business, you'll enter into financial agreements with lenders. These agreements specify the terms of the loan, including interest rates, repayment schedules, and collateral requirements.

 Legal Review of Contracts

It's advisable to have legal counsel review any contractual agreements to ensure that your interests are protected and that the terms are fair and compliant with relevant laws.

Understanding and adhering to these contractual agreements is vital for maintaining positive relationships with location owners, suppliers, and service providers, which, in turn, is essential for the success of your vending machine business.

❖ **Case Study: Health Bites Vending's Regulatory Compliance**

To illustrate the importance of legal and regulatory compliance, let's explore a case study of "Health Bites Vending," a successful vending machine business that prioritized compliance and customer safety.

Case Study: Health Bites Vending

Health Bites Vending, owned by Sarah, specializes in offering healthy snack and beverage options in various locations, including schools, fitness centres, and hospitals. Sarah recognized the need for strict compliance with regulations to ensure the safety and health of her customers.

Licensing and Permits: Sarah diligently obtained all the necessary licenses and permits for her vending machine business, including a general business license, health department permits, and sales tax permits. She also adhered to state-specific requirements, such as nutritional guidelines for vending machines in schools.

Product Labelling and Nutrition Information: Health Bites Vending worked with suppliers who provided accurate and compliant product labelling, including nutrition facts labels and allergen information. The vending machines displayed calorie information prominently as required by law.

Product Safety and Quality Standards: Sarah established rigorous procedures for maintaining the safety and quality of her products. Regular inspections, temperature monitoring, and adherence to food safety regulations were paramount.

Compliance with Accessibility Laws: Health Bites Vending ensured that its vending machines were accessible to all customers. Sarah made modifications to the machines to accommodate customers with disabilities and provided clear signage.

Data Privacy and Security: The company implemented robust data security measures, especially in handling customer data and cashless payments. Compliance with data privacy laws was a top priority.

Contractual Agreements: Health Bites Vending carefully reviewed and negotiated contractual agreements with property owners, suppliers, and service providers to protect its interests and ensure compliance.

Insurance Coverage: Sarah secured comprehensive insurance coverage to protect her business from unexpected events and liabilities. This included general liability insurance, product liability insurance, and cybersecurity insurance.

Food and Beverage Regulations: The company strictly adhered to food and beverage regulations, including food safety, food labelling, and health department inspections.

Environmental Considerations: Health Bites Vending adopted environmentally friendly practices, such as using energy-efficient vending machines and implementing recycling programs.

Taxes and Financial Compliance: The company maintained accurate financial records, reported income and sales tax appropriately, and consulted with tax professionals to ensure compliance.

Competition and Antitrust Laws: While not a major concern for a small business like Health Bites

Vending, the company remained aware of competition and antitrust laws to ensure fair and ethical business practices.

Vandalism and Security: Sarah's company implemented security measures on its vending machines and promptly addressed any security concerns to prevent vandalism and theft.

As a result of its commitment to compliance, Health Bites Vending earned a reputation for safety, transparency, and customer trust, contributing to its success in the vending machine industry.

❖ **Key Takeaways**

In this chapter, you've explored the legal and regulatory considerations essential for running a successful vending machine business. Here are the key takeaways:

1. Obtain the necessary licenses and permits, including business licenses, vending machine operator licenses, health department permits, and sales tax permits.

2. Comply with product labelling and nutrition information requirements, including Nutrition Facts labels and allergen disclosure.

3. Maintain product safety and quality standards to ensure customer safety and satisfaction.

4. Adhere to accessibility laws to make your vending machines accessible to all customers, including those with disabilities.

5. Implement strong data privacy and security

measures to protect customer information and comply with data privacy laws.

6. Review and negotiate contractual agreements carefully to protect your business interests when working with property owners, suppliers, and service providers.

7. Obtain the appropriate insurance coverage to protect your business from various risks and liabilities.

8. Comply with food and beverage regulations, including food safety, labeling, and health department inspections, if you sell food and beverages.

9. Consider environmental practices and sustainability to reduce your business's environmental footprint and appeal to eco-conscious customers.

10. Ensure compliance with tax laws and reporting requirements, including sales tax collection, income tax, and other tax obligations.

11. Stay aware of competition and antitrust laws, especially if your business grows and operates in multiple locations.

12. Implement security measures and insurance coverage to protect your vending machines from vandalism and security breaches.

By addressing these legal and regulatory considerations, you can build a vending machine business that not only operates smoothly and profitably but also prioritizes customer safety, transparency, and environmental responsibility.

Chapter 5: Sourcing Products, Negotiating Deals, and Inventory Management

In the vending machine business, the success of your venture heavily relies on the products you offer. Finding the right suppliers, negotiating favourable deals, and managing your inventory efficiently are critical aspects of running a profitable vending machine business.

❖ Sourcing Products

Sourcing the right products is the foundation of your vending machine business. To provide what your target audience desires, you need to identify reliable suppliers and products that align with your customers' preferences. Here's how to go about it:

1. Identify Your Target Market

Before you source products, you must understand your target market. Determine the demographics, preferences, and dietary requirements of the customers at each vending machine location. Are they health-conscious individuals, busy professionals, students, or gym-goers? This information will guide your product selection.

2. Research Suppliers

Once you know your target market, start researching suppliers that can provide products that cater to their needs. Consider the following types of suppliers:

Wholesalers: Wholesalers offer a wide range of

products at bulk prices. They are a cost-effective option for stocking your vending machines with popular snacks and beverages.

Local Distributors: Local distributors may specialize in specific product categories or brands. Building relationships with local distributors can be beneficial, especially if you require specialized or regional products.

Direct from Manufacturers: In some cases, you might be able to source products directly from manufacturers. This is common for specialized or unique products. Contact manufacturers to inquire about bulk pricing and distribution options.

Vending Machine-Specific Suppliers: Some suppliers specialize in products tailored for vending machines. These products are often packaged and priced for convenience.

3. Product Variety

Offering a diverse product range can attract a broader customer base. Consider stocking various categories of products, such as snacks, beverages, healthy options, and special dietary products. Keep in mind the preferences of your target market at each location.

4. Quality and Freshness

Customers expect freshness and quality. Choose suppliers that provide fresh and well-packaged products. Regularly check product expiration dates and remove items that are close to expiration from your vending machines.

5. Sample Products

Before committing to a supplier, request product samples. This allows you to assess the taste, quality, and packaging of the products. It's essential to ensure that the products meet your standards and the preferences of your target audience.

6. Negotiate Terms

Once you've identified potential suppliers and sampled their products, it's time to negotiate terms. Negotiations can cover various aspects, including pricing, delivery schedules, and minimum order quantities. **Here are some negotiation tips:**

- Pricing: Seek competitive pricing, especially if you plan to purchase products in bulk. Volume discounts can be advantageous. Be

- prepared to negotiate for favorable pricing, but also consider the quality of the products.

- Payment Terms: Discuss payment terms with your suppliers. Some may offer discounts for early payment, while others may allow net-30 or net-60 payment terms. Understand the financial implications of these terms for your business.

- Delivery Schedules: Determine a delivery schedule that aligns with your restocking needs. Timely deliveries are crucial to maintaining a well-stocked vending machine.

- Minimum Order Quantities: Suppliers may have minimum order quantities. Negotiate these quantities based on your business's

- needs to avoid overstocking or running out of products.

- Quality Assurance: Discuss quality assurance measures with your suppliers. Understand their processes for product quality control, packaging, and handling.

- Exclusive Agreements: In some cases, you might negotiate exclusive agreements with suppliers for specific product categories. This can give your vending machine business a competitive edge.

7. Supplier Agreements

Once negotiations are complete, formalize your arrangements with suppliers through supplier agreements. These agreements should detail the terms and conditions of your business relationship, including pricing, delivery schedules, quality standards, and dispute resolution procedures.

❖ Inventory Management

Efficient inventory management is crucial to ensure that your vending machines are consistently stocked with fresh products. Proper inventory management helps prevent product wastage and ensures that you meet customer demand. Here's how to effectively manage your inventory:

1. Inventory Tracking System

Implement an inventory tracking system to monitor product levels in your vending machines. This can be done manually or through vending management software, which offers real-time tracking and reporting.

2. Regular Audits

Conduct regular audits of your vending machines to check for product availability, product condition, and any maintenance issues. These audits should be scheduled based on the traffic and demand at each location.

3. Restocking Schedule

Establish a restocking schedule that aligns with the consumption patterns of your customers. High-traffic locations may require more frequent restocking, while lower-traffic locations may have a more extended restocking interval.

4. FIFO Method

Implement the "first in, first out" (FIFO) method. This means that the oldest products should be placed at the front of the machine, ensuring that products with shorter shelf lives are sold first.

5. Expiration Date Monitoring

Continuously monitor product expiration dates. Remove items that are close to expiration and replace them with fresh products. Selling expired products not only damages your reputation but may also have legal consequences.

6. Forecasting and Data Analysis

Use historical sales data to forecast future demand. This can help you adjust your inventory levels and product mix accordingly. Vending management software often provides valuable data for this purpose.

7. Preventing Theft and Tampering

Protect your inventory from theft or tampering.

Ensure that your vending machines are secure, and consider installing security cameras in high-risk locations.

8. Supplier Communication

Maintain open communication with your suppliers. Inform them of any changes in demand or special promotions so they can adjust their deliveries accordingly.

9. Storage Conditions

Store your inventory in suitable conditions to maintain product freshness. Be mindful of temperature-sensitive products and ensure they are stored at the right temperature.

10. Product Rotation

Implement a regular product rotation strategy. Move products from one slot to another to ensure all products have a chance to sell.

11. Equipment Maintenance

Regularly maintain your vending machines to ensure that they function correctly. Malfunctions or breakdowns can result in product spoilage and lost revenue.

12. Reducing Waste

Minimize waste by donating unsold but still fresh products to local charities or organizations. This not only reduces waste but also fosters a positive image for your business in the community.

13. Recycle Packaging

Encourage recycling by providing recycling bins near your vending machines, especially if you offer products with recyclable packaging.

14. Technology Solutions

Consider investing in vending machine management software that offers real-time inventory tracking, sales data analysis, and predictive maintenance alerts. This technology can significantly streamline your inventory management process.

Effective inventory management ensures that your vending machines are consistently stocked with the products your customers desire, reduces product waste, and contributes to the profitability of your business.

❖ Case Study: FreshChoice Vending

To illustrate effective sourcing, negotiation, and inventory management, let's delve into a case study of "FreshChoice Vending," a successful vending machine business that prioritizes quality and efficiency.

Case Study: FreshChoice Vending

FreshChoice Vending, owned by David, operates vending machines across a wide range of locations, from office buildings to universities and hospitals.

David's approach to sourcing products, negotiating deals, and inventory management has been instrumental in his business's success.

Sourcing Products:

David recognizes that sourcing the right products is a

pivotal aspect of his vending machine business. He starts by thoroughly understanding the needs and preferences of the customers at each location. For instance, at a university, he caters to students with a mix of healthy snacks, energy drinks, and study-friendly snacks, while at an office building, he stocks premium coffee, light meals, and healthier options.

He has established relationships with a variety of suppliers, including local distributors for snacks, a coffee supplier for office locations, and a beverage wholesaler for drinks. This diverse network of suppliers allows him to offer a wide array of products while maintaining quality.

Negotiating Deals:

David's negotiation skills have been key to securing favorable terms with his suppliers. He has worked to ensure competitive pricing with volume discounts where applicable. For coffee and specialty beverages, he negotiates for exclusive agreements with suppliers to provide unique products not found in competing vending machines.

He's also transparent about his expectations, ensuring that delivery schedules align with the restocking needs of each location. David understands the importance of maintaining good relations with his suppliers to guarantee the continued availability of products.

Inventory Management:

FreshChoice Vending has a robust inventory management system. David uses vending management software to monitor product levels in real-time. Regular audits are conducted based on location traffic and consumption patterns. High-traffic locations are audited more frequently, while lower-traffic locations have less frequent audits.

He diligently follows the FIFO method, ensuring that the oldest products are sold first. Expiration date monitoring is a top priority to avoid selling expired products. David uses historical sales data to forecast demand and adjust inventory levels accordingly.

To prevent theft and tampering, he invests in secure vending machines and strategically places security cameras in high-risk locations. His open communication with suppliers allows him to inform them of any changes in demand or special promotions, ensuring that deliveries are tailored to the specific needs of each location.

David's commitment to efficient inventory

management not only minimizes waste but also contributes to the consistent availability of fresh and desirable products in his vending machines.

In summary, sourcing products, negotiating deals, and effectively managing inventory are critical components of a successful vending machine business. By understanding your target audience, establishing strong supplier relationships, and implementing robust inventory management practices, you can ensure that your vending machines consistently offer appealing products and generate consistent revenue.

Chapter 6: Vending Machine Maintenance, Repairs, and Cleaning

Vending machines are a convenient and profitable business venture, but their reliability and functionality are essential for success. Regular maintenance, quick repairs, and diligent cleaning are key aspects of keeping your vending machines running smoothly and ensuring customer satisfaction. In this chapter, we'll delve into the intricacies of vending machine maintenance, repairs, and the importance of regular cleaning and restocking.

Basic Maintenance and Repairs

Vending machines, like any mechanical equipment, require routine maintenance and occasional repairs to ensure they function correctly. Here's how to handle basic maintenance and repairs:

1. Regular Inspections

Frequent inspections are essential for identifying any issues with your vending machines. Create a checklist of items to inspect, including the coin mechanism, bill validator, product delivery system, and refrigeration unit (if applicable).

2. Cleaning and Sanitization

Regular cleaning is crucial to maintain the appearance and hygiene of your vending machines. Clean both the exterior and interior of the machines. Pay special attention to product delivery trays, coin slots, and buttons. Use food-safe cleaning products to prevent any potential contamination.

3. Stock Rotation

Implement the "first in, first out" (FIFO) method for

product rotation. This ensures that the oldest products are dispensed first, reducing the chances of products going stale or expiring.

4. Restocking

Maintain a restocking schedule based on the consumption patterns of your customers. Oversee the inventory to ensure you have enough products to meet demand. Timely restocking is vital for keeping your machines operational and profitable.

5. Component Lubrication

Regularly lubricate moving components like coils, motors, and hinges to prevent excessive wear and tear. Follow the manufacturer's recommendations for lubrication intervals and use appropriate lubricants.

6. Change Coin Tubes and Bill Validators

Empty coin tubes and bill validators regularly to prevent jams or malfunctions. Replace full coin tubes and ensure that bill validators are in working order.

7. Lighting and Display Checks

Verify that all lighting elements and digital displays are functioning correctly. Replace any burnt-out bulbs or malfunctioning LED displays promptly.

8. Button Calibration

Calibrate the machine's selection buttons to ensure they respond accurately to customer inputs. Buttons that don't function properly can frustrate customers and lead to lost sales.

9. Regular Technical Training

If you have on-site personnel responsible for vending

machine maintenance, ensure they receive regular technical training from the machine's manufacturer or distributor. This helps them troubleshoot and address common issues effectively.

10. Record Keeping

Maintain detailed records of all maintenance and repairs. Note the date, the issue, and the actions taken. This documentation can help identify recurring problems and guide future maintenance efforts.

Handling Technical Issues

Vending machines can encounter various technical issues over time. Addressing these issues promptly is essential to prevent disruptions in your business. Here are common technical issues and how to handle them:

1. Coin or Bill Validator Jams

Coin and bill validator jams can occur when customers insert coins or bills incorrectly or when the mechanisms become clogged. **Here's how to handle these jams:**

- Turn off the machine to prevent further damage.

- Open the machine's access panel to reach the coin and bill validators.

- Carefully remove any jammed coins or bills.

- Inspect the validators for any visible obstructions or damage.

- Clean and lubricate the validators.

- Test the validators to ensure they're working correctly before closing the access panel and restarting the machine.

2. Product Delivery Problems

Issues with the product delivery system can lead to frustrated customers. **If products aren't dispensing correctly or consistently, follow these steps:**

- Power off the machine and open the access panel to the product delivery area.

- Check for any obstructions or jammed products in the delivery system.

- Inspect product coils or spirals for misalignment or damage.

- Clean the delivery mechanism and ensure it's lubricated.

- Test the product delivery system by selecting different items to verify that they dispense properly.

3. Refrigeration Failures

For vending machines that offer refrigerated products, refrigeration failures can result in spoiled items. **If you notice issues with temperature control:**

- Power off the machine and open the access panel to the refrigeration unit.

- Check for any visible damage to the refrigeration components.

- Clean the condenser coils to ensure proper airflow.

- Verify that the thermostat or temperature settings are correctly adjusted.

- If the refrigeration system still doesn't function correctly, contact a professional technician or the manufacturer for repairs.

4. Electrical Problems

Electrical issues can range from minor glitches to complete power failures. **Here's how to handle electrical problems:**

- Ensure the machine is powered off before inspecting electrical components.

- Check the power cord and outlet for any visible damage or loose connections.

- Inspect the machine's internal wiring for loose or frayed connections.

- Use a multimeter to test the power supply and components for continuity.

- If you can't identify or resolve the issue, contact a qualified technician to diagnose and repair the electrical problem.

5. Display and Selection Button Malfunctions

Issues with the machine's display or selection buttons can deter customers. **If these components aren't working correctly:**

- Turn off the machine to prevent further damage.

- Inspect the display and buttons for physical damage or loose connections.

- Clean the display and buttons with a soft, dry cloth.

- Recalibrate the selection buttons if necessary.

- If the issue persists, consult the manufacturer or a technician to address the problem.

6. Cash Handling Problems

Cash handling issues, such as coins not being

accepted or bills not being validated, can frustrate customers. **To address these problems:**

- Turn off the machine and open the access panel to the cash handling components.

- Inspect the coin and bill validators for damage or obstructions.

- Ensure that the coin and bill pathways are clear and clean.

- Test the validators with different denominations to verify their functionality.

- If the issue persists, consult the manufacturer or a technician with expertise in cash handling systems.

 7. Vandalism or Tampering

Vending machines are sometimes subject to vandalism or tampering. These actions can damage the machine or compromise its security. **To address**

vandalism or tampering:

- Inspect the machine for signs of physical damage or forced entry.

- Review any security camera footage if available.

- Report any incidents to the local authorities and document the damage.

- Repair any structural or cosmetic damage promptly.

- Consider installing security measures, such as tamper-evident seals or security cameras, to deter future incidents.

8. Internet Connectivity Issues

If your vending machine is equipped with internet connectivity for inventory tracking and remote monitoring, connectivity issues can disrupt your business. **To address internet connectivity problems:**

- Check the machine's Wi-Fi or cellular connection for signal strength.

- Ensure that login credentials are correct and that the machine is connected to the right network.

- Restart the machine to refresh the connection.

- Consult with your vending machine provider or IT support for assistance in resolving connectivity issues.

9. Power Outages and Interruptions

Power outages or interruptions can temporarily disrupt your vending machine operations. **To handle power-related issues:**

- Check the power source and verify that it's stable.

- If the power issue is external (e.g., a building-wide power outage), wait for power to be restored.

- Ensure that your vending machine has surge protection in place to prevent damage from power surges.

- If the power outage is frequent or specific to the machine, consult an electrician to assess and resolve the issue.

10. Alarm Notifications

Many modern vending machines are equipped with alert systems that can notify you of technical issues. **If you receive an alert or notification:**

- Review the alert message to understand the issue.

- Inspect the machine in person or remotely (if supported) to identify the problem.

- Address the issue following the appropriate

troubleshooting steps or by contacting a technician if needed.

Handling technical issues promptly is essential to maintain the functionality and profitability of your vending machines. Regular inspections and maintenance can help prevent many common issues, but having a plan in place for addressing problems when they arise is equally important.

❖ **Regular Cleaning and Restocking**

In addition to maintenance and repairs, regular cleaning and restocking are vital for the overall success of your vending machine business. Here's how to effectively manage cleaning and restocking:

Cleaning Procedures

Exterior Cleaning: Wipe down the exterior of your

vending machines regularly to maintain a clean and attractive appearance. Use a mild, food-safe cleaning solution to remove dust, fingerprints, and stains.

Interior Cleaning: Clean the interior of the vending machine, including product trays, coils, and delivery mechanisms. Pay close attention to areas where food or beverages may spill or accumulate.

Product Trays: Remove and clean product trays as needed. Wash them with warm, soapy water and ensure they're thoroughly dry before returning them to the machine.

Coin Mechanism and Bill Validator: Periodically clean the coin mechanism and bill validator to prevent dirt or grime buildup. Use a soft, dry cloth to wipe these components gently.

Button and Touchscreen Cleaning: Clean the selection buttons or touchscreen with a soft, dry cloth or a mild screen cleaning solution. Avoid using abrasive materials that can scratch the display.

Condenser Coils: If your vending machine has refrigeration, clean the condenser coils regularly to maintain optimal cooling efficiency. Refer to the manufacturer's guidelines for cleaning procedures.

Restocking Procedures

Restocking Schedule: Create a restocking schedule that aligns with the consumption patterns of your customers at each location. High-traffic locations may require more frequent restocking, while lower-traffic locations may need less frequent attention.

Inventory Monitoring: Monitor inventory levels through your inventory management system or vending machine management software. Set alerts to notify you when specific products are running low.

Product Rotation: Continuously follow the FIFO method to ensure that the oldest products are sold first. Regularly check for expired or nearly expired items and remove them from the machine.

Fresh Product Availability: Make sure that fresh and high-demand products are consistently available. This includes snacks, beverages, and any perishable items.

Product Variety: Offer a diverse product range to cater to a wide range of customer preferences. Periodically assess the product mix and make adjustments as needed.

Seasonal Offerings: Introduce seasonal or limited-time offerings to keep your product selection fresh and appealing. Consider holiday-themed products or seasonal snacks.

Restocking Efficiency: Train your restocking personnel to work efficiently. Ensure they are familiar with the vending machine layout and know where to find products quickly.

Supplier Communication: Maintain open communication with your suppliers to ensure timely deliveries and address any product availability issues.

Effective cleaning and restocking procedures not only contribute to a positive customer experience but also help prevent product spoilage and maximize your vending machine's profitability.

❖ Case Study: Reliable Vend Solutions

To exemplify the significance of vending machine maintenance, repairs, cleaning, and restocking, let's explore a case study of "Reliable Vend Solutions," a vending machine business known for its commitment to exceptional service.

Case Study: Reliable Vend Solutions

Reliable Vend Solutions, operated by Sarah, provides vending machine services to various locations, including corporate offices, schools, and healthcare facilities. Sarah has built a reputation for delivering reliable and well-maintained vending machines.

Maintenance and Repairs:

Sarah prioritizes maintenance and promptly

addresses any technical issues. She conducts regular inspections of her vending machines to identify potential problems. Her approach includes training her staff in basic maintenance tasks, such as cleaning, product rotation, and button calibration.

In cases of technical issues, Sarah acts swiftly. She maintains a close relationship with the manufacturer, allowing her to access technical support when needed. Her record-keeping system helps track recurring issues and find solutions proactively.

Cleaning and Restocking:

Sarah's commitment to cleanliness is evident in the impeccable appearance of her vending machines. She follows a rigorous cleaning schedule, ensuring that both the exterior and interior of the machines are free from dirt, stains, and odors.

She has also implemented an efficient restocking system. Sarah relies on inventory management software to monitor stock levels and receive notifications when products are running low. Her restocking personnel are well-trained, and they follow a structured schedule to ensure timely replenishment.

In addition to regular restocking, Sarah introduces seasonal offerings and rotates product selections to keep her machines fresh and appealing to customers. The combination of meticulous maintenance, quick repairs, thorough cleaning, and efficient restocking has earned Reliable Vend Solutions a reputation for delivering exceptional service and a hassle-free vending experience for customers.

Sarah's proactive approach to vending machine maintenance has not only minimized technical issues but has also reduced downtime and revenue loss. Her attention to detail in cleaning and restocking keeps customers coming back for more.

In summary, vending machine maintenance, repairs, cleaning, and restocking are essential practices to ensure the smooth operation and profitability of your vending machine business. By conducting regular inspections, addressing technical issues promptly, and maintaining high standards of cleanliness, you can create a positive customer experience and maintain the reliability of your vending machines.

Chapter 7: Pricing Strategies for Your Vending Machine Business

Pricing is a critical aspect of your vending machine business. Setting the right prices for your products, understanding profit margins, and implementing effective price adjustments can greatly influence your business's success. In this chapter, we'll delve into the intricacies of pricing strategies tailored to the vending machine industry.

❖ Setting the Right Prices for Your Products

Pricing your vending machine products appropriately is a delicate balance. You want to offer competitive prices that attract customers while ensuring that your business remains profitable. Here's how to set the right prices for your products:

1. Product Cost Analysis

Begin by analyzing the cost of each product you offer in your vending machines. This includes the cost of purchasing the product, any taxes or fees, and the cost of stocking and maintaining the vending machine.

2. Profit Margin Calculation

Determine your desired profit margin. This margin represents the difference between the cost of the product and the price at which you intend to sell it. Profit margins can vary depending on your business goals, but a common approach is to aim for a 40-50% margin.

3. Competitive Analysis

Research the prices of similar products in your local market. Knowing what competitors charge for similar items can help you set prices that are competitive and attractive to your customers.

4. Location-Specific Pricing

Consider varying your prices based on the location of your vending machines. High-traffic areas with captive audiences, such as office buildings or schools, may support slightly higher prices. In contrast, lower-traffic locations might require more competitive pricing to attract customers.

5. Price Sensitivity

Understand the price sensitivity of your target audience. Some locations may be more price-sensitive than others, so be prepared to adjust your pricing accordingly.

6. Bundle Deals

Offer bundle deals or combo pricing for customers

who purchase multiple items. For example, you can provide a discount for customers who buy a snack and a beverage together.

7. Seasonal Pricing

Consider seasonal pricing adjustments. You might raise prices slightly during peak seasons or lower them during slower periods to maintain consistent sales.

8. Special Promotions

Run periodic promotions or discounts on specific products or categories. Limited-time offers can create excitement and encourage more significant purchases.

9. Convenience Pricing

Some customers are willing to pay a premium for the convenience of vending machine products. Factor this into your pricing strategy, especially if your machines are in convenient locations.

10. Feedback and Testing

Gather feedback from customers about your pricing. You can do this through surveys or by analyzing sales data. Experiment with different price points to see how they impact sales and adjust accordingly.

11. Customer Loyalty Programs

Implement a customer loyalty program that rewards frequent customers with discounts or special offers. This can encourage repeat business.

12. Regular Review

Periodically review and adjust your pricing strategy to reflect changes in the market, customer preferences, and your business goals. Being adaptable is crucial to staying competitive.

❖ Understanding Profit Margins

Profit margins are a vital component of pricing strategies in the vending machine business. Understanding profit margins allows you to set prices that ensure profitability while remaining competitive. Here's a breakdown of profit margins and how they impact your pricing:

Gross Profit Margin

The gross profit margin is the difference between the cost of goods sold (COGS) and the revenue generated from product sales.

Net Profit Margin

The net profit margin takes into account all expenses, including operating costs, overhead, and taxes, to provide a more comprehensive view of your profitability.

While the gross profit margin focuses solely on the cost of goods sold, the net profit margin gives you a clearer picture of the overall profitability of your business.

Understanding your profit margins is essential for making informed pricing decisions. It helps you assess the financial health of your vending machine business and identify opportunities to improve profitability.

❖ **Implementing Price Adjustments**

Pricing adjustments are necessary to adapt to changing market conditions, customer preferences, and business goals. Implementing price adjustments effectively can help you maintain competitiveness and profitability. **Here's how to handle price adjustments:**

1. Market Research

Regularly conduct market research to stay informed about changes in consumer behavior, competitor pricing, and emerging product trends. This information will guide your price adjustments.

2. Data Analysis

Analyze sales data to identify product performance trends. Pay attention to which products are selling well and which might be underperforming. Data can reveal valuable insights about your pricing strategy.

3. Customer Feedback

Gather feedback from customers about pricing. Customer surveys or feedback mechanisms on your vending machines can provide insights into customer perceptions of your prices.

4. Competitor Analysis

Monitor the pricing strategies of your competitors. If you notice that similar products are consistently priced lower, consider adjusting your prices to remain competitive.

5. Seasonal Adjustments

Leverage seasonal pricing adjustments. For example, you can offer discounts or promotions during holidays or special events to attract more customers.

6. Regular Review

Set a schedule for regularly reviewing and adjusting your prices. This could be on a quarterly or semi-annual basis, depending on your business's needs.

7. A/B Testing

Consider running A/B tests with different price points for select products to gauge customer reactions. This allows you to experiment with pricing without committing to widespread changes.

8. Dynamic Pricing

Implement dynamic pricing for certain products. This strategy involves adjusting prices in real-time based on demand, time of day, or other factors. Vending machine management software can assist in implementing dynamic pricing.

9. Bundle and Combo Pricing

Offer bundle and combo pricing to encourage customers to purchase more items. This can include discounts when customers buy multiple products together.

10. Customer Loyalty Discounts

Reward loyal customers with discounts or special pricing. A loyalty program that offers reduced prices to frequent purchasers can foster customer retention.

11. Test Incremental Changes

When making price adjustments, consider incremental changes rather than drastic shifts. Small price increases or decreases are less likely to deter customers or disrupt your business.

12. Monitor the Impact

After implementing price adjustments, closely monitor their impact on sales and profitability. Use your sales data and financial reports to evaluate the effectiveness of the changes.

13. Communicate Changes

If you make significant price adjustments, consider communicating them to customers in advance. This can help manage expectations and reduce potential negative reactions.

14. Competitive Positioning

Position your vending machine business competitively within the market. Evaluate your unique selling points and consider how pricing can be used to your advantage.

15. Flexibility

Stay flexible in your approach to pricing. The vending machine business is dynamic, and your pricing strategy should evolve to meet changing circumstances.

Case Study: Savvy VendCo Pricing

To illustrate effective pricing strategies in the vending machine business, let's explore a case study of "Savvy VendCo," a successful vending machine company known for its innovative pricing approach.

Case Study: Savvy VendCo

Savvy VendCo, led by Alex, operates vending machines in various locations, including corporate offices, fitness centers, and schools. Alex's approach to pricing has been instrumental in the company's success.

Market Research and Data Analysis:

Alex prioritizes market research and data analysis to stay ahead of the competition. He regularly conducts surveys and collects customer feedback through the vending machines. This data helps him understand customer preferences and their willingness to pay for different products.

Using vending machine management software, Alex tracks product performance, identifies trends, and adjusts pricing based on the data. He pays particular attention to high-selling items and fine-tunes their prices to optimize profitability.

Dynamic Pricing:

Savvy VendCo has implemented dynamic pricing for select products. For instance, the price of certain snacks may vary based on the time of day or the day of the week. Alex's vending management software allows him to adjust prices in real-time to maximize revenue during peak hours.

Bundle and Combo Pricing:

To encourage larger purchases, Alex offers bundle and combo pricing. Customers who buy a bottle of water and a snack, for example, receive a discount on the combined purchase. This strategy not only increases the average transaction value but also enhances customer satisfaction.

Customer Loyalty Discounts:

Savvy VendCo has a customer loyalty program that rewards frequent customers with discounts. Customers who make multiple purchases receive a digital card that provides discounts on subsequent transactions. This encourages repeat business and customer retention.

Regular Price Reviews:

Alex conducts quarterly price reviews to ensure that Savvy VendCo remains competitive. He analyzes sales data, reviews customer feedback, and evaluates the company's overall financial performance. This regular review process enables him to make informed pricing decisions.

Effective Communication:

When Savvy VendCo makes significant price adjustments, Alex communicates the changes to customers in advance. He uses signage on the vending machines and digital notifications to inform customers about upcoming adjustments. This transparency has been well-received by customers.

By incorporating these pricing strategies, Savvy

VendCo has maintained a strong position in the market while continuously improving profitability and customer satisfaction.

In conclusion, setting the right prices, understanding profit margins, and implementing effective price adjustments are crucial components of a successful vending machine business. By staying informed about market trends, customer preferences, and competitor pricing, you can make informed pricing decisions that maximize profitability while delivering value to your customers.

.

Chapter 8: Business Operations for Your Vending Machine Business

Successful business operations are the backbone of your vending machine business. This chapter delves into the core aspects of operating your business effectively, including route planning and scheduling, cash management and security, and providing top-notch customer service and communication.

❖ Route Planning and Scheduling

Efficient route planning and scheduling are essential for maximizing the profitability of your vending machine business. Here's how to manage this crucial aspect effectively:

1. Location Assessment

Begin by assessing the locations where your vending

machines are placed. Understand the traffic patterns, peak hours, and customer preferences at each location.

2. Route Optimization

Organize your routes to minimize travel time and fuel expenses. Prioritize locations that are geographically close to each other and plan routes to avoid backtracking.

3. Scheduling Frequency

Determine how frequently each location should be serviced. High-traffic areas may require daily or bi-weekly visits, while lower-traffic locations may be serviced less often.

4. Timing Considerations

Consider the timing of your visits to coincide with peak customer traffic. For example, service locations with breakfast items in the morning and focus on snack and beverage machines during afternoon breaks.

5. Maintenance and Restocking

Schedule maintenance and restocking as part of your routes. This ensures that all vending machines are well-maintained, stocked, and in good working condition.

6. Technology Tools

Utilize route optimization software and mobile apps to streamline route planning and scheduling. These tools can help you save time and reduce fuel costs.

7. Backup Plans

Have contingency plans in place for unexpected events like vehicle breakdowns or traffic delays. Consider partnering with a local repair service for quick assistance.

Regular Review

Regularly review and fine-tune your route planning and scheduling to adapt to changes in customer behavior and location dynamics. Flexibility is key to optimal route management.

❖ Cash Management and Security

Cash management and security are paramount in the vending machine business, as it involves handling cash transactions. Here's how to handle these aspects with care:

1. Cash Collection Procedure

Establish a secure cash collection procedure. Specify who is responsible for collecting cash from each machine, when collections should occur, and the method for transporting cash to a secure location.

2. Safes and Cash Handling Equipment

Invest in high-quality safes or secure cash handling equipment to store cash between collections. These should be located in a secure area with limited access.

3. Collection Records

Maintain detailed records of cash collections from each machine. This includes the date, time, amount collected, and the machine's location. Accurate records are essential for financial transparency.

4. Cashless Payment Options

Offer cashless payment options, such as credit card readers or mobile payment apps, to reduce the amount of cash handled. Cashless payments are not only convenient for customers but also enhance security.

5.Training and Security Protocols

Train your employees on cash handling procedures and security protocols. Ensure that they understand the importance of security and follow best practices.

6.Security Measures

Implement security measures to protect your vending machines from theft or vandalism. This may include security cameras, alarms, and tamper-evident seals.

7.Regular Cash Deposits

Make regular cash deposits at a financial institution to reduce the amount of cash kept on hand. This minimizes the risk of theft or loss.

8.Insurance Coverage

Consider insurance coverage for theft, vandalism, or cash losses. Having the appropriate insurance can provide financial protection in case of unforeseen events.

9.Vendor Support

Some vending machines have built-in security features, such as bill and coin acceptors with anti-fraud technology. Partner with reputable vending machine suppliers who prioritize security.

❖ Customer Service and Communication

Excellent customer service and effective communication can set your vending machine business apart from the competition. **Here's how to excel in these areas:**

1. Machine Maintenance and Cleanliness

Regularly maintain and clean your vending machines to ensure that they are in optimal working condition and present an appealing appearance to customers.

2. Product Variety and Freshness

Offer a diverse product selection, including healthy options and popular brands. Ensure that products are fresh and not past their expiration dates.

3. Responsive Customer Support

Provide a contact number or email for customers to report issues or request assistance. Respond promptly to customer inquiries and resolve issues efficiently.

4. Clear Pricing Information

Display pricing information prominently on or near your vending machines. Transparent pricing eliminates confusion and fosters trust with customers.

5. Refund and Return Policies

Establish clear refund and return policies. If a

customer receives a damaged product or faces issues with a purchase, make it easy for them to receive a refund or replacement.

6. Communication Channels

Maintain open communication channels with your customers. Use social media, email newsletters, or text alerts to inform customers about promotions, new products, or changes in your business.

7. Customer Feedback Collection

Gather feedback from customers about their preferences, product requests, and satisfaction with your service. This valuable information can guide improvements in your offerings.

8. Regular Surveys

Periodically conduct customer surveys to assess your vending machines' performance and gather insights for enhancements. Incentivize participation with discounts or promotions.

9. Responsive to Trends

Stay responsive to market trends and customer demands. Adjust your product offerings and pricing based on changing preferences.

10 Customer Loyalty Programs

Implement a customer loyalty program that rewards frequent customers with discounts or special offers. A loyalty program can foster customer retention and increased sales.

11. Regular Customer Appreciation

Show appreciation to your customers through occasional promotions or discounts. Celebrate holidays and special occasions with themed offerings.

12. Training for Staff

Train your staff to provide excellent customer service. Encourage a friendly and helpful attitude when interacting with customers.

13. Community Engagement

Engage with the local community by supporting events or sponsoring activities. Being an active member of the community can enhance your brand's reputation.

14. Social and Environmental Responsibility

Consider incorporating social and environmental responsibility into your business practices. This may include sourcing sustainable products or supporting charitable initiatives.

15. Emergency Response Plan

Develop an emergency response plan for situations like vending machine malfunctions or product recalls. Ensure that your team is prepared to address these situations promptly.

❖ Case Study: Stellar Vending Services

To illustrate effective business operations, customer service, and communication, let's explore a case study of "Stellar Vending Services," a leading vending machine business known for its outstanding customer-centric approach.

Case Study: Stellar Vending Services

Stellar Vending Services, led by Lisa, has earned a reputation for providing exceptional customer service and maintaining high operational standards.

Machine Maintenance and Cleanliness:

Stellar Vending Services conducts regular maintenance and cleaning of its vending machines. Lisa's team adheres to a strict cleaning schedule, ensuring that all machines are in pristine condition. The machines are not only functional but also a delight to use.

Product Variety and Freshness:

Lisa takes pride in offering a diverse product selection. She stays updated on consumer trends and preferences, adding new items to meet changing demands. The products are regularly checked for freshness, and expired items are promptly replaced.

Responsive Customer Support:

Stellar Vending Services provides a dedicated customer support line for inquiries and issues. Lisa's team is trained to respond quickly and professionally to address customer concerns.

Clear Pricing Information:

Each vending machine is equipped with clearly displayed pricing information, eliminating any ambiguity. Customers can make informed decisions, and there are no surprises at the point of purchase.

Refund and Return Policies:

The company has well-defined refund and return policies. In case of a damaged or unsatisfactory purchase, customers can expect a hassle-free refund or replacement process.

Customer Feedback Collection:

Stellar Vending Services actively collects customer feedback through online surveys and feedback mechanisms on its vending machines. This feedback is used to make improvements and cater to customer preferences.

Responsive to Trends:

Lisa closely follows market trends and customer demands. If a particular product gains popularity or a new dietary trend emerges, she's quick to incorporate these offerings into her vending machines.

Customer Loyalty Programs:

Stellar Vending Services has a successful customer loyalty program. Frequent customers receive a loyalty card that offers discounts and exclusive promotions, encouraging repeat business.

Regular Customer Appreciation:

Lisa celebrates holidays and special occasions by offering themed promotions and discounts to her customers. These initiatives are well-received and create a sense of community around her vending machines.

Training for Staff:

Lisa places a strong emphasis on training her staff to deliver excellent customer service. Her team is friendly and helpful, ensuring that customers have a positive experience.

Community Engagement:

Stellar Vending Services actively engages with the local community. The company sponsors community events and participates in charitable initiatives, strengthening its ties to the area.

Social and Environmental Responsibility:

Lisa integrates social and environmental responsibility into her business practices. She sources sustainable and ethically produced products and supports local charitable causes.

Emergency Response Plan:

The company has a well-defined emergency response plan for machine malfunctions or product recalls. Lisa's team is prepared to respond swiftly to any situation that may arise.

By focusing on customer service, communication, and effective business operations, Stellar Vending Services has set itself apart as a leader in the vending machine industry. The company's commitment to customer satisfaction and community engagement has been integral to its success.

In summary, efficient route planning and scheduling, rigorous cash management and security measures, and a dedication to top-notch customer service and communication are essential elements of running a successful vending machine business. By addressing these aspects with care and attention, you can create a thriving business that delights customers and operates seamlessly.

Chapter 9: Marketing and Promotion for Your Vending Machine Business

Marketing and promotion are the keys to expanding your vending machine business and reaching a broader audience. In this chapter, we will explore the core aspects of marketing, including developing a brand and logo, online and offline marketing strategies, and effective methods for attracting new customers and retaining existing ones.

❖ Developing a Brand and Logo

A strong brand identity sets your vending machine business apart and helps build trust with your customers.

Here's how to develop a compelling brand and logo:

1. Brand Identity

- Define your brand's identity by considering the values, mission, and unique selling points of your vending machine business. What sets you apart from the competition?

- Understand your target audience and what appeals to them. Your brand should resonate with your customers.

2. Brand Name

- Choose a memorable and relevant name for your business. It should be easy to pronounce, spell, and remember.

- Ensure that the name is not already in use or trademarked by another business. Conduct a thorough name search.

3. Logo Design

- Design a professional and eye-catching logo that represents your brand. The logo should be simple, versatile, and easily recognizable.

- Consider working with a professional graphic designer who can bring your brand vision to life.

4. Color Palette and Typography

- Select a color palette that reflects your brand's personality. Different colors evoke different emotions, so choose wisely.

- Choose typography (fonts) that align with your brand's character. Typography should be legible and harmonize with your logo.

5. Brand Messaging

- Create a clear and compelling brand message that communicates what your business is about. This message should be consistent across all marketing materials.

- Craft a compelling brand story that connects with your customers on a personal level. Share your journey and values.

6. Consistency

- Maintain consistency in your branding across all marketing channels. This includes your website, social media, vending machine designs, and promotional materials.

- Consistency builds brand recognition and trust. Your customers should instantly recognize your brand.

Online and Offline Marketing Strategies

Effective marketing strategies encompass both online and offline approaches. **Here are strategies for promoting your vending machine business:**

Online Marketing:

1. Website Development:

- Create a professional website for your vending machine business. Include information about your products, locations, and contact details.

- Optimize your website for search engines (SEO) to improve visibility on search results pages.

2. Social Media Marketing:

- Establish a presence on social media platforms such as Facebook, Instagram, and Twitter. Share engaging content, including images of your vending machines and promotions.

- Interact with your audience, respond to comments and messages, and build a sense of community.

3. Email Marketing:

- Build an email list of customers interested in updates, promotions, and new products. Send regular newsletters with valuable content and offers.

- Personalize your emails to cater to different customer segments and preferences.

4. Content Marketing:

- Create blog posts, articles, or videos related to vending machine products, healthy snacking, or customer success stories.

- Share informative content on your website and social media channels to position your brand as an authority in the vending industry.

5. Online Advertising:

- Invest in online advertising campaigns such as Google Ads or social media ads. Target specific demographics to reach potential customers effectively.

- Monitor the performance of your online ads and adjust your strategy based on the results.

6. Review Management:

- Encourage satisfied customers to leave positive reviews on platforms like Google, Yelp, or social media.

- Respond promptly to negative reviews and address customer concerns professionally and constructively.

Offline Marketing:

1. Vending Machine Design:

- Design your vending machines with eye-catching graphics and branding elements that make them stand out in the location.

- Consider themed or seasonal machine designs to attract attention.

2. Brochures and Flyers:

- Create brochures or flyers that highlight your vending machine offerings and benefits. Distribute them in high-traffic areas.

- Include contact information and a call to action to encourage inquiries or sales.

3. Local Partnerships:

- Build partnerships with local businesses, schools, and offices to place your vending machines in their facilities.

- Collaborate on promotions or special discounts for their employees or customers.

4. Sampling Events:

- Organize sampling events where customers can try new products from your vending machines.

- Engage with potential customers directly and gather feedback.

5. Billboards and Signage:

- Use billboards or signage at strategic locations to create brand visibility. These can be particularly effective in high-traffic areas.

- Ensure that your branding and message are clear and easy to read.

6. Community Involvement:

- Participate in community events, sponsor local sports teams or charity events, and support neighborhood initiatives.

- Being an active member of the community builds trust and goodwill.

❖ **Attracting New Customers and Retaining Existing Ones**

Attracting new customers while retaining existing ones is a delicate balance.

Here's how to effectively manage both aspects of customer relations:

Attracting New Customers:

1. Special Promotions:

- Offer special promotions or discounts to new customers who try your vending machines for the first time.

- Highlight these promotions on your website and social media to attract attention.

2. Referral Programs:

- Implement a referral program that rewards existing customers who refer new clients to your vending machines.

- Offer incentives such as discounts or free products for successful referrals.

3. Location Analysis:

- Continuously seek out new high-traffic locations for your vending machines. Conduct market research to identify untapped areas.

- Establish partnerships with location owners to secure placements in their facilities.

4. Customer Demographics:

- Understand the demographics of your target customers. Tailor your products and marketing messages to cater to their preferences and needs.

- Monitor trends and adjust your offerings accordingly.

5. Mobile Apps:

- Develop a mobile app that allows customers to locate your vending machines easily and access exclusive offers or loyalty rewards.

- Ensure that the app is user-friendly and regularly updated.

6. Customer Feedback:

- Gather feedback from customers about their preferences and expectations. Use this information to make adjustments to your offerings and services.

- Act on customer feedback promptly to demonstrate that you value their opinions.

Retaining Existing Customers:

1. Loyalty Programs:

- Implement a customer loyalty program that rewards repeat customers with discounts, free products, or exclusive offers.

- Encourage customers to return to your vending machines to benefit from the loyalty program.

2. Regular Communication:

- Keep existing customers engaged by sending regular newsletters, emails, or text alerts. Inform them of new products, promotions, and updates.

- Share valuable content that enhances their experience.

3. Feedback Collection:

- Continue gathering feedback from existing customers to assess their satisfaction levels and expectations.

- Make improvements based on their feedback to show that you are responsive to their needs.

4. Personalized Offers:

- Personalize offers and promotions for existing customers based on their purchase history and preferences.

- Send personalized recommendations and offers that align with their previous buying patterns.

5. Community Engagement:

Engage with your local community and existing

customers through events, sponsorships, or participation in charitable initiatives.

Show that you are a supportive and active member of the community.

6. Regular Machine Maintenance:

Maintain your vending machines to ensure they remain in optimal working condition. A malfunctioning machine can frustrate customers and deter repeat business.

Keep machines clean, well-stocked, and visually appealing.

7. Quick Issue Resolution:

Address any customer concerns or issues promptly and professionally. Make it easy for customers to reach out and resolve problems.

Ensure that customers have a positive experience

even when things go wrong.

8. Surprise and Delight:

Occasionally surprise your existing customers with unexpected promotions or free products. Create moments that delight and reward their loyalty.

These gestures foster a strong sense of customer appreciation.

9. Social Responsibility:

Engage in social and environmental responsibility initiatives, demonstrating your commitment to making a positive impact on society.

Share your initiatives with your customers, allowing them to be a part of the positive change.

❖ Case Study: VendoPro Marketing Mastery

To illustrate effective marketing and customer retention strategies, let's explore a case study of "VendoPro Marketing Mastery," a vending machine business known for its marketing excellence.

Case Study: VendoPro Marketing Mastery

VendoPro Marketing Mastery, led by Mark, is renowned for its innovative marketing strategies and commitment to customer satisfaction.

Attracting New Customers:

Mark conducts regular special promotions to attract new customers to his vending machines. He offers "First-Timer Discounts," where customers receive a significant discount on their first purchase.

He implemented a referral program that rewards existing customers with a free product every time they refer a new customer who makes a purchase. This program has generated a consistent flow of new customers.

By using location analysis and market research, Mark has expanded his vending machine network into previously untapped locations, further increasing his customer base.

Retaining Existing Customers:

VendoPro Marketing Mastery has a comprehensive customer loyalty program that provides customers with a loyalty card. Frequent customers earn points for every purchase, which can be redeemed for discounts and exclusive offers.

Mark communicates with existing customers through regular newsletters and emails. He provides updates on new products, promotions, and even invites them to participate in customer surveys.

Through personalized offers, Mark tailors promotions for existing customers based on their past purchases. For example, if a customer frequently buys healthy snacks, Mark sends them exclusive discounts on healthy products.

Community Engagement:

Mark actively engages with the local community by sponsoring local sports events and supporting charitable causes. Customers appreciate that VendoPro Marketing Mastery is a responsible member of the community.

The company is committed to social responsibility by offering a selection of sustainable and ethically sourced products. Mark communicates these initiatives to customers, making them feel that they are part of a positive change.

Surprise and Delight:

To delight existing customers, Mark occasionally includes surprise free products in their purchases. Customers love the unexpected bonuses and feel appreciated.

Quick Issue Resolution:

VendoPro Marketing Mastery has a responsive customer support team that addresses customer concerns swiftly and professionally. This dedication to problem-solving ensures a positive customer experience.

Regular Machine Maintenance:

Mark's team maintains vending machines meticulously. They ensure that all machines are clean, well-stocked, and visually appealing.

This commitment to machine upkeep keeps customers satisfied.

Social Media and Online Marketing:

The company maintains active social media profiles and a well-designed website that informs customers about products, promotions, and the company's community involvement.

Online advertising campaigns, such as targeted Google Ads, have helped VendoPro Marketing Mastery reach new customers and drive traffic to its vending machines.

By implementing these marketing and customer retention strategies, VendoPro Marketing Mastery has solidified its position as a marketing leader in the vending machine industry. The company continuously attracts new customers while keeping existing ones engaged and satisfied.

In conclusion, developing a strong brand identity and logo, combining effective online and offline marketing strategies, and focusing on both attracting new customers and retaining existing ones are key components of promoting your vending machine business. With the right marketing approaches, you can expand your reach, build customer loyalty, and ensure the long-term success of your business.

Chapter 10: Scaling Your Vending Business

Scaling your vending machine business involves expanding and growing your operations. In this chapter, we will explore essential strategies for scaling your business, including expanding your vending machine fleet, diversifying product offerings, and exploring franchising opportunities.

❖ **Expanding Your Vending Machine Fleet**

Expanding your vending machine fleet is one of the most straightforward ways to scale your business. **Here are steps to consider:**

1. Location Research

- Conduct thorough location research to identify high-traffic areas where new vending machines can be placed.

- Analyze data from your existing machines to determine which products are the most popular. This data can guide your decisions when selecting new locations.

2. New Machine Selection

- Choose vending machines that align with the preferences and needs of the target audience at the new location.

- Consider factors like size, capacity, and payment options when selecting new machines.

3. Location Agreements

- Establish agreements with location owners or managers. Ensure the terms are mutually

- beneficial and cover aspects like commission rates and maintenance responsibilities.

- Communicate your plans for regular machine maintenance, restocking, and any special promotions to attract customers.

4. Sourcing Funding

- Evaluate your financial situation and determine whether you need additional funding to acquire new machines and cover operational costs.

- Consider options like business loans, partnerships, or reinvesting profits from your existing vending machines.

5. Installation and Setup

- Properly install and set up your new vending machines. Ensure they are in optimal working condition and that the product assortment is appealing to customers.

- Train your staff on the new machine's operation, maintenance, and restocking.

6. Marketing and Promotion

- Promote the new vending machines to attract customers. Use both online and offline marketing strategies to create awareness.

- Consider special promotions or discounts for the first few weeks to encourage trial and build a customer base.

7. Data Collection and Analysis

- Continuously collect data from your new vending machines to track their performance. This includes sales data, customer feedback, and machine status reports.

- Use this data to adjust your offerings and strategies to optimize profitability.

8. Scalability Plan

- Develop a scalability plan that outlines how many new machines you intend to add over a specific period.

- Consider regional expansion, targeting new cities or areas where your business can grow.

❖ Diversifying Product Offerings

Diversifying your product offerings can attract a wider customer base and increase sales. Here's how to approach this:

1. Customer Preferences

Gather data and insights about customer preferences. Conduct surveys and analyze sales data to identify products that customers are looking for.

Explore trends in snacking, health-conscious products, and dietary restrictions to cater to a diverse range of preferences.

2. Product Selection

Research and select new products to add to your vending machines. Consider healthy snacks, organic options, or niche products that are in demand.

Ensure that the products you choose align with your

target audience's preferences.

3. Supplier Relationships

Build strong relationships with suppliers and distributors. Negotiate favorable terms and agreements for sourcing new products.

Look for suppliers that offer unique and exclusive items that can set your vending machines apart.

4. Inventory Management

Implement effective inventory management practices to ensure that products are fresh and do not expire. Regularly rotate products to prevent staleness.

Use vending machine management software to monitor product performance and identify slow-moving items.

5. Pricing Strategy

Adjust your pricing strategy to accommodate

different product price points. Offer competitive pricing while maintaining profitability.

Bundle products or offer combo deals to encourage customers to try new items.

6. Product Promotion

Promote new products through marketing campaigns and signage on your vending machines. Create excitement and curiosity around these items.

Consider offering free samples or limited-time promotions for new products to encourage customer trials.

7. Customer Feedback

Gather feedback from customers about the new products. Use this information to make adjustments, discontinue underperforming items, and introduce products that customers request.

Act on customer feedback to demonstrate that you are responsive to their needs and preferences.

❖ Franchising Opportunities

Franchising can be an effective way to scale your vending machine business. Here are the key steps and considerations:

1. Franchise Development Plan

Develop a comprehensive franchise development plan that outlines your objectives, target markets, and business model for potential franchisees.

Determine the initial franchise fee and ongoing royalty or licensing fees.

2. Legal and Regulatory Compliance

Ensure that your franchise business complies with all legal and regulatory requirements. Seek legal counsel to establish the necessary agreements, contracts, and disclosure documents.

Familiarize yourself with franchising laws specific to your region or country.

3. Franchisee Selection and Training

Select franchisees who share your vision and values. Look for individuals who are dedicated, motivated, and capable of running a vending machine business.

Provide comprehensive training and support to franchisees, covering vending machine operation, product selection, inventory management, and customer service.

4. Brand Consistency

Maintain brand consistency across all franchise locations. Ensure that your brand identity, logo, and quality standards are upheld in each vending machine business.

Implement brand guidelines and regular audits to ensure consistency.

5. Marketing Support

Offer marketing support to franchisees to help them promote their vending machine businesses effectively.

Provide access to marketing materials, strategies, and best practices.

Collaborate on national or regional marketing campaigns to build brand awareness.

6. Continuous Support

Establish ongoing support and communication channels with franchisees. Offer assistance with troubleshooting, product selection, and business development.

Create a network or community where franchisees

can share insights and experiences.

7. Franchise Growth Strategy

Develop a strategy for franchise growth that outlines how you will expand your network. Consider regional expansion or targeting specific types of locations.

Ensure that you have the resources and infrastructure to support a growing franchise network.

8. Franchisee Relationship Management

Foster positive relationships with franchisees through open communication, regular meetings, and feedback collection.

Address concerns or challenges promptly and professionally to maintain a strong franchisee relationship.

9. Legal and Financial Support

Provide franchisees with guidance on legal and financial matters related to their businesses, such as tax compliance, insurance, and financial management. Offer access to financial resources or support for acquiring vending machines and product inventory.

❖ Case Study: VendoScape Franchising Success

Let's explore a case study of "VendoScape," a vending machine business that successfully expanded through franchising.

Case Study: VendoScape

VendoScape, led by Sarah, is a vending machine business that expanded through franchising. The company specializes in healthy snacks and innovative product offerings.

Franchise Development Plan:

Sarah developed a franchise development plan that outlined her vision for VendoScape franchises. She focused on high-traffic locations, such as corporate offices and fitness centers, as prime franchise opportunities.

Legal and Regulatory Compliance:

Sarah ensured that VendoScape complied with all legal and regulatory requirements for franchising. She worked with legal experts to create franchise agreements and disclosure documents.

Franchisee Selection and Training:

VendoScape carefully selected franchisees who shared the company's vision for healthy snacking and customer satisfaction. Franchisees underwent rigorous training, learning how to operate vending machines efficiently and provide top-notch customer service.

Brand Consistency:

VendoScape maintained strict brand consistency, ensuring that the company's logo, branding elements, and quality standards were upheld in all franchise locations.

Marketing Support:

The company offered marketing support to franchisees, providing access to marketing materials, strategies, and guidance on local marketing campaigns.

Continuous Support:

VendoScape established ongoing support channels

with franchisees, including a dedicated support team and regular meetings to address challenges and share best practices.

Franchise Growth Strategy:

The company followed a franchise growth strategy that focused on regional expansion. Sarah identified areas with high demand for healthy snacks and targeted those locations.

Franchisee Relationship Management:

Sarah maintained strong relationships with franchisees, fostering open communication and addressing concerns promptly. She valued the insights and experiences of franchisees and encouraged collaboration.

Legal and Financial Support:

VendoScape offered franchisees guidance on legal

and financial matters, ensuring that they were well-equipped to manage their businesses.

Through effective franchising, VendoScape experienced significant growth, expanding its network of franchise locations and establishing itself as a leader in the healthy vending machine industry.

In conclusion, scaling your vending machine business involves expanding your vending machine fleet, diversifying your product offerings, and exploring franchising opportunities. These strategies can help you reach new markets, attract a wider customer base, and expand your business network. By carefully planning and executing each aspect, you can position your vending machine business for sustained growth and success.

Chapter 11: Challenges and Pitfalls in the Vending Machine Industry

While operating a vending machine business can be a rewarding and profitable venture, it is not without its challenges and pitfalls. In this chapter, we will explore common issues in the vending machine industry and provide guidance on how to handle setbacks and challenges effectively.

Common Issues in the Vending Machine Industry

1. Machine Malfunctions and Technical Issues: Vending machines, like any mechanical device, can experience technical problems. These issues can lead to revenue losses and customer dissatisfaction.

Solution: Implement regular maintenance schedules

and have a responsive maintenance team to address issues promptly. Consider investing in vending machine management software that can monitor machine status and send alerts in case of malfunctions.

2. Stale or Expired Products:

Over time, products in vending machines can become stale or expire. This not only results in wasted inventory but can also damage your reputation with customers.

Solution: Implement a strict inventory management system, regularly check expiration dates, and rotate products to ensure the freshest offerings. Monitor product performance and discontinue items that consistently underperform.

3. *Competition and Location Challenges:*

Competition can be fierce in the vending machine industry, and securing high-traffic locations can be a challenge.

Solution: Conduct thorough location research and build strong relationships with location owners or managers. Offer unique products or services that set your vending machines apart from the competition.

4. *Cash Management and Security:*

Handling cash can pose security risks, and vending machines are susceptible to vandalism or theft.

Solution: Implement secure cash management practices, including regular collections and bank deposits. Consider transitioning to cashless payment options, such as card readers or mobile payment systems, to reduce the risk associated with cash transactions.

5. Product Theft or Tampering:

Some customers may attempt to steal or tamper with vending machine products, causing financial losses.

Solution: Implement security measures, such as anti-theft technology or surveillance cameras, to deter theft. Monitor machines regularly and address tampering promptly.

6. Changing Consumer Preferences:

Consumer preferences can shift over time, affecting the popularity of certain products. Failing to adapt to changing preferences can lead to declining sales.

Solution: Stay attuned to market trends and conduct customer surveys to understand evolving preferences.

Adjust your product offerings accordingly and introduce new items that cater to current trends.

7. Regulatory Compliance:

The vending machine industry is subject to various regulations, including health and safety standards. Non-compliance can result in fines and legal issues.

Solution: Stay informed about local, state, and federal regulations that pertain to your vending machines. Ensure that your machines meet all safety and health requirements. Consult legal experts if necessary.

8. Product Spoilage in Refrigerated Machines:

If you operate refrigerated vending machines, the risk of products spoiling due to equipment malfunctions or power outages is a concern.

Solution: Regularly maintain and service

refrigerated machines to prevent breakdowns. Invest in backup power sources, such as generators or battery backups, to protect perishable products.

9. Vandalism and Graffiti:

Vandalism and graffiti can deface vending machines, causing damage to the machine's exterior and reducing its appeal to customers.

Solution: Place vending machines in well-lit and secure locations to deter vandalism. Consider using anti-graffiti coatings and regularly clean and maintain the machines.

10. Economic Downturns:

Economic downturns can affect consumer spending, resulting in reduced sales for vending machine businesses.

Solution: Diversify your product offerings to include

budget-friendly options that appeal to cost-conscious customers. Offer promotions and discounts during challenging economic times to maintain customer interest.

❖ **How to Handle Setbacks and Challenges**

Facing setbacks and challenges in the vending machine industry is inevitable. However, how you respond to these challenges can determine your success. Here are strategies for effectively handling setbacks:

1. Stay Proactive:

Regularly monitor the performance of your vending machines and address issues as soon as they arise. Develop contingency plans for potential challenges, such as machine malfunctions or location changes.

2. Invest in Maintenance and Training:

Allocate resources to regular maintenance and staff training. Well-maintained machines are less likely to malfunction, and knowledgeable staff can address technical issues and provide excellent customer service.

3. Customer Communication:

Maintain open communication with customers. Address their concerns and issues promptly and professionally. Make it easy for customers to reach out and provide feedback.

4. Adapt to Market Changes:

Keep an eye on market trends and consumer preferences. Be ready to adjust your product offerings, pricing strategies, and promotions to align with changing market dynamics.

5. Networking and Collaboration:

Build a network within the vending machine industry. Collaborate with other vending operators to share insights and experiences. Collective knowledge can help you navigate challenges more effectively.

6. Legal and Regulatory Compliance:

Stay informed about the legal and regulatory requirements that apply to your vending machines. Consult legal experts to ensure compliance and handle any legal issues professionally.

7. Diversification and Innovation:

Continuously innovate and diversify your product offerings. Introduce new and exciting products that capture customer interest and adapt to changing preferences.

8. Security and Risk Mitigation:

Implement security measures to protect your machines from theft, tampering, and vandalism. Invest in insurance to mitigate financial risks associated with certain challenges.

9. Financial Planning:

Maintain a robust financial plan and budget. Set aside funds for contingencies and unexpected expenses. A solid financial buffer can help you weather financial setbacks.

10. Customer Service Excellence:

Deliver outstanding customer service. Positive interactions with customers can mitigate the impact of challenges and help build customer loyalty.

11. Market Analysis and Location Selection:

Continuously analyze your market and the performance of your vending machines. If a location consistently underperforms, consider relocating to a more promising area.

12. Adapt to Technology:

Embrace technology to streamline operations and enhance customer experiences. Implement cashless payment options and vending machine management software for efficiency.

13. Stress Management:

Running a business can be stressful, especially when challenges arise. Implement stress management techniques, and consider seeking support or counseling if necessary.

❖ Case Study: Overcoming Challenges

Let's examine a case study of a vending machine business that effectively overcame common industry challenges.

Case Study: VendSmart Solutions

VendSmart Solutions, led by Alex, operates vending machines in various locations, including schools, offices, and gyms. The business faced several challenges but managed to overcome them.

Machine Malfunctions and Technical Issues:

Alex invested in a vending machine management software that alerted his team to machine malfunctions promptly. They established a routine maintenance schedule, ensuring that machines remained in optimal condition.

Changing Consumer Preferences:

VendSmart regularly surveyed its customers to gauge product preferences. Alex introduced healthier snack options, which aligned with evolving consumer preferences for healthier snacking.

Economic Downturns:

During economic downturns, VendSmart offered budget-friendly snack bundles and promotions to maintain customer interest. These initiatives helped mitigate the impact of reduced consumer spending.

Vandalism and Graffiti:

VendSmart Solutions experienced some instances of vandalism, especially in school locations. To address this, Alex collaborated with school administrations to improve security and deter vandalism. He also used anti-graffiti coatings and ensured that the machines were regularly cleaned and maintained.

Security and Risk Mitigation:

Alex invested in security measures, including surveillance cameras and machine alarms, to protect the machines from theft and tampering. Additionally, he had insurance in place to mitigate the financial risks associated with these challenges.

Market Analysis and Location Selection:

VendSmart constantly analyzed location performance. If a vending machine consistently underperformed, the team considered relocating to more promising areas. This approach helped optimize the placement of vending machines.

Adapt to Technology:

The company embraced technology by implementing cashless payment options and vending machine management software. This not only improved operational efficiency but also enhanced the customer experience.

Customer Service Excellence:

VendSmart prioritized outstanding customer service. Alex and his team were responsive to customer inquiries and concerns. Positive customer interactions helped build customer loyalty.

Financial Planning:

The business maintained a strong financial plan, setting aside funds for contingencies and unexpected expenses. Having a financial buffer proved crucial in dealing with financial setbacks.

By proactively addressing these challenges and adapting to changing circumstances, VendSmart Solutions not only overcame common industry issues but also managed to thrive in a competitive market.

Operating a vending machine business can be a rewarding endeavor, but it comes with its share of challenges and pitfalls. By understanding the common issues in the vending machine industry and adopting proactive strategies for handling setbacks, you can increase your chances of success. Stay vigilant, adapt to market changes, prioritize customer service, and invest in technology to navigate challenges effectively and build a resilient and thriving vending machine business.

Chapter 12: Future Trends in Vending

The vending machine industry is evolving rapidly, driven by technological advancements, changing consumer preferences, and a growing emphasis on sustainability. In this chapter,

❖ Technological Advancements in Vending

Vending machines have come a long way since their inception, and they continue to evolve with technological innovations. The integration of advanced technology is enhancing user experience, operational efficiency, and even expanding the types of products that can be offered through vending machines.

Here are some notable technological trends:

1. Cashless Payment Options:

The shift towards cashless payment methods is a prominent trend. Vending machines now commonly accept mobile payments, credit and debit cards, and digital wallets. This not only provides convenience to customers but also reduces the risk associated with handling cash.

2. Touchless Interfaces:

Touchless interfaces, such as touchscreen displays and gesture recognition, are becoming more prevalent. These interfaces offer a hygienic and interactive way for customers to make their selections.

3. Artificial Intelligence (AI) and Machine Learning:

AI and machine learning are being utilized to optimize inventory management. Predictive algorithms can analyze sales data and product trends, enabling vending operators to restock machines more efficiently and reduce product wastage.

4. Internet of Things (IoT) Integration:

Vending machines are increasingly connected through IoT technology. This connectivity allows operators to remotely monitor machine status, receive real-time data, and even implement automatic troubleshooting.

5. Personalization and Recommendations:

Some vending machines are now equipped with facial

recognition or biometric technology to recognize individual customers. This enables personalized product recommendations based on past preferences and purchasing history.

6. Remote Management and Analytics:

Vending operators can access real-time data and machine analytics remotely through cloud-based systems. This allows for better management and decision-making, reducing downtime and improving overall performance.

7. Sustainable Power Options:

Some vending machines are being designed to run on renewable energy sources, such as solar power. This reduces their environmental footprint and supports sustainability efforts.

❖ Sustainability and Eco-Friendly Vending Options

The vending machine industry is increasingly embracing sustainability and eco-friendly practices. Consumers are becoming more conscious of their environmental impact, and vending operators are responding to these concerns. **Here are some key trends in this area:**

1. Green Vending Machines:

Many vending machine manufacturers are incorporating eco-friendly features into their designs. This includes using energy-efficient LED lighting, low-energy refrigeration, and eco-friendly refrigerants to reduce power consumption and greenhouse gas emissions.

2. Biodegradable Packaging:

Vending machines are offering products with biodegradable packaging. Snacks and beverages in compostable containers reduce waste and minimize the environmental impact of vending.

3. Sustainable Sourcing:

Vending operators are sourcing products from suppliers with strong sustainability practices. This includes products made from ethically sourced ingredients and fair trade practices.

4. Recycling Initiatives:

Some vending machines are equipped with recycling capabilities. Customers can deposit their used containers into the machine, which compacts and stores them for recycling.

5. Promoting Refillable Containers:

Vending operators are encouraging customers to use their refillable containers. This not only reduces single-use packaging waste but also promotes sustainability.

6. Locally Sourced Products:

The trend of offering locally sourced products through vending machines is gaining traction. This reduces the carbon footprint associated with transporting products over long distances.

7. Green Initiatives in Machine Placement:

Vending operators are working with location partners to implement sustainability initiatives. For example, placing vending machines in locations powered by renewable energy sources or encouraging waste recycling on-site.

8. Sustainable Materials:

Vending machine exteriors are being made with sustainable and recycled materials. Manufacturers are increasingly conscious of their environmental impact and strive to reduce it through their designs.

❖ Case Study: SustainableSips Vending

SustainableSips Vending, led by Emily Stevens, is a vending machine business that specializes in eco-friendly and sustainable beverage options. The company has been at the forefront of sustainability in the vending industry.

Case Study: SustainableSips Vending

Emily Stevens, the founder of SustainableSips Vending, has been committed to offering eco-friendly beverage options since the inception of her business.

Q: Emily, what inspired you to create SustainableSips Vending?

Emily: I've always had a passion for environmental conservation, and I wanted to bring sustainability into the vending machine industry. I saw an opportunity to provide customers with beverages that had a minimal environmental impact.

Q: What are some key sustainable practices you've implemented in your vending business?

Emily: We focus on several sustainability practices, including using energy-efficient vending machines that run on solar power. We also offer a range of beverages in recyclable and biodegradable packaging. Promoting refillable containers is another major initiative for us.

Q: How have customers responded to your sustainability efforts?

Emily: Customers have been incredibly supportive. They appreciate the transparency of our sustainability practices and are enthusiastic about reducing their own environmental impact. Our recycling initiatives have been particularly well-received.

Q: Can you share any memorable moments from your journey with SustainableSips Vending?

Emily: One memorable moment was when we received recognition for our eco-friendly vending machines from a local environmental organization. It was a proud moment for our team and a testament to our commitment to sustainability.

Q: What advice do you have for vending operators looking to embrace sustainability?

Emily: My advice is to start with small, meaningful changes that align with your values and your customers' preferences. Sustainable practices can be gradually incorporated into your operations. It's important to be transparent about your efforts and to educate your customers on how they can participate in sustainability initiatives.

The vending machine industry is entering a new era of technological advancement and sustainability. Operators who embrace the latest technology trends are better positioned to provide enhanced customer experiences, streamline operations, and offer a wider range of products. Additionally, the

increasing emphasis on sustainability and eco-friendly vending options aligns with the growing awareness of environmental concerns.

As you explore opportunities in the vending machine industry, consider how you can leverage technology to improve your operations and offer innovative products. Moreover, think about how you can implement sustainability practices and eco-friendly options in your vending business to meet the demands of environmentally conscious customers.

Chapter 13: Conclusion

In the journey of exploring the world of vending machines, we've covered a wide array of topics, from the inception of your vending business to the latest technological advancements and sustainability initiatives. Now, as we conclude this comprehensive guide, let's take a moment to recap the key takeaways and offer encouragement and tips for aspiring vending entrepreneurs.

Recap of Key Takeaways

1. Start with a Solid Plan:

Your journey in the vending machine industry begins with a well-thought-out business plan. This plan should encompass your goals, budget, location choices, and product selections.

2. Location is Key:

The success of your vending machines heavily depends on their placement. Seek high-traffic areas and build strong relationships with location owners or managers.

3. Diversify Your Product Offerings:

Embrace variety in your vending machines. Consider the preferences of your target audience and offer a mix of snacks, beverages, and other products.

4. Maintenance is Crucial:

Regular maintenance is essential for keeping your vending machines in optimal condition. Well-maintained machines are less likely to experience technical issues.

5. Pricing Strategies Matter:

Setting the right prices for your products requires a balance between profitability and customer satisfaction. Regularly review and adjust your pricing strategies to stay competitive.

6. Customer Service is Paramount:

Providing excellent customer service is key to retaining customers and building a loyal customer base. Be responsive, attentive, and professional in all interactions.

7. Market and Promote Your Business:

Develop a brand identity and utilize various marketing strategies to attract new customers and keep your business visible. Both online and offline marketing play crucial roles.

8. Scale Your Business Carefully:

When you're ready to expand, consider options such as adding more vending machines, diversifying your product offerings, and exploring franchising opportunities.

9. Embrace Technology:

The vending industry is witnessing significant technological advancements, including cashless payment options, touchless interfaces, AI, and IoT integration. These innovations can enhance your operations and customer experience.

10. Prioritize Sustainability:

Embracing sustainability practices, such as using eco-friendly vending machines, sourcing sustainable products, and promoting recycling, can align your business with the growing demand for environmentally conscious solutions.

❖ Encouragement and Tips for Aspiring Vending Entrepreneurs

For those who are considering venturing into the vending machine industry, here are some words of encouragement and valuable tips:

1. Believe in Your Vision:

Your passion and belief in your vending business will be your driving force. Have confidence in your vision, and let it guide your decisions and actions.

2. Differentiate Your Offerings:

To stand out in a competitive market, offer something unique or of higher quality. Diversify your product selections and continually seek innovative options.

3. Be Persistent and Patient:

Building a successful vending business takes time. Don't be discouraged by initial setbacks or challenges. Persevere and stay committed to your goals.

4. Build Strong Relationships:

The vending industry is as much about relationships as it is about machines and products. Cultivate strong partnerships with location owners and suppliers.

5. Learn Continuously:

Stay curious and open to learning. The vending industry evolves, and keeping up with the latest trends and technologies will give you a competitive edge.

6. Prioritize Customer Experience:

Your customers are the heart of your business. Ensure they have positive experiences with your vending machines, and go the extra mile to exceed their expectations.

7. Plan for Sustainability:

As environmental awareness grows, integrating sustainability practices into your business is not just a trend; it's a necessity. Plan for eco-friendly options from the beginning.

8. Network and Collaborate:

Building a network within the vending industry can provide valuable insights and support. Collaborate with other vending operators to share experiences and best practices.

9. Explore New Locations:

Don't hesitate to explore new and unique locations for your vending machines. The right location can significantly impact your success.

10. Stay Resilient:

Running a vending machine business can be challenging, but resilience is a key trait of successful entrepreneurs. Embrace setbacks as learning opportunities and keep moving forward.

11. Celebrate Milestones:

Celebrate your successes, both big and small. Acknowledge your achievements and use them as motivation to set new goals.

12. Plan for the Future:

Consider exit strategies and succession planning for

your vending business. Having a clear vision for the future will provide you with a sense of direction.

As you embark on your journey in the vending machine industry, remember that each day is an opportunity to learn, grow, and make a positive impact. You have the potential to bring innovation, convenience, and sustainability to the lives of your customers.

I hope this guide has equipped you with the knowledge and inspiration to take your first steps or continue your path as a successful vending entrepreneur. Whether you're offering gourmet snacks, healthy options, or indulgent treats, your vending business can bring joy and satisfaction to people's lives. Embrace the opportunities, challenges, and trends that come your way, and build a vending business that thrives for years to come.

I wish you the best of luck in your vending machine journey. Your success in this industry is not just a possibility; it's a vending machine away!